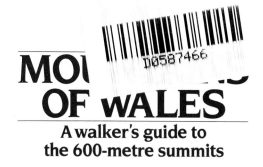

MO[ ]

OF wALES

**A walker's guide to
the 600-metre summits**

Also by Terry Marsh

The Summits of Snowdonia

British Library Cataloguing in Publication Data
Marsh, Terry
  The mountains of Wales: a walker's guide
  to the 600-metre summits.
  1. Mountains – Wales – Guide-books
  2. Wales – Description and travel – 1981- –
  Guide-books
  I. Title
  914.29′04858   DA735
  ISBN 0-340-34827-5

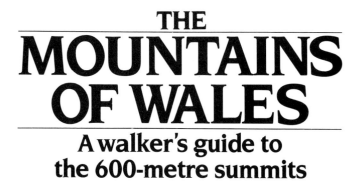

THE
MOUNTAINS
OF WALES

A walker's guide to
the 600-metre summits

TERRY MARSH

HODDER AND STOUGHTON
LONDON SYDNEY AUCKLAND TORONTO

FOR FRANCES

Acknowledgments

I am indebted to my friend Allan Rimmer who read the draft manuscript for me, and who followed in my footsteps across a number of the hills, offering helpful advice. I owe especial thanks to Tim Owen in the Ordnance Survey at Southampton, who gave a lot of time to checking all the heights and map references. And I am grateful to the staff of the Library Service of Wigan, who produced all the books I needed for reference. The staff of the Ordnance Survey Record Map Library were also most helpful in making all the maps (and space to consult them in peace and quiet) available to me.

I am obliged to Herbert Carr for permission to quote from *The Mountains of Snowdonia*; and to Esme Kirby, Chairperson of the Snowdonia National Park Society, for quotations from her work, and the comments she made on sections of the book.

All the photographs are mine, but the task of performing darkroom magic with what I brought back from the hills has been undertaken by Len Hudson LRPS, to whom I am grateful.

Finally, I owe a great debt of gratitude to Frances, to whom the book is dedicated, who accompanied me on every trip to the hills, provided (sometimes unwillingly) the human figure to give scale to some of the photographs, read through the draft and proofs with me, and more than once encouraged me to keep going.

T.M.

Contents

KEY TO SECTIONS

1 Snowdon and Eilio
2 Glyders
3 Carneddau
4 Hebog and Nantlle
5 Siabod and the Moelwyns
6 Rhinogs
7 Arenigs

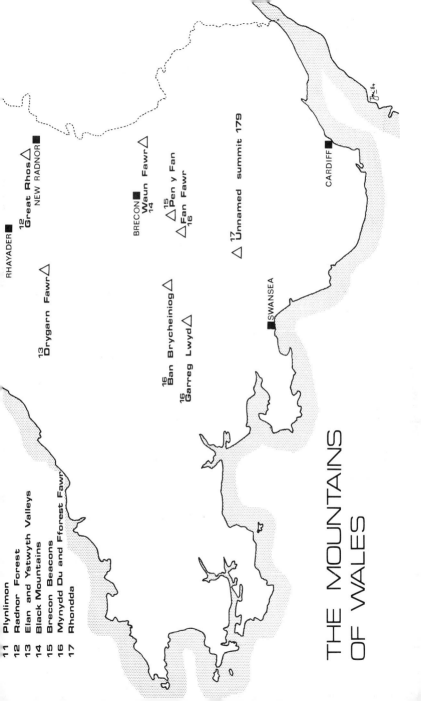

THE MOUNTAINS
OF WALES

11 Plynlimon
12 Radnor Forest
13 Elan and Ystwyth Valleys
14 Black Mountains
15 Brecon Beacons
16 Mynydd Du and Fforest Fawr
17 Rhondda

RHAYADER ■

12 Great Rhos △
NEW RADNOR ■

13 Drygarn Fawr △

BRECON ■
Waun Fawr △
14
15 △ Pen y Fan
△ Fan Fawr
16

16 Ban Brycheiniog △

16 Garreg Lwyd △

17 △ Unnamed summit 179

SWANSEA ■

CARDIFF ■

Introduction

Not long after I moved to live in North Wales, and before even starting the job which had taken me there in the first place, I was on the hills. From my living-room window the Carneddau and Glyder ranges spread themselves invitingly across the horizon. How could such provocation be ignored? Snowdon, almost inevitably, was first. Then came excursions into the Carneddau and the Glyders. Only a few months of weekend walking later every mountain in North Wales had been visited. Or so I thought, because by this time, having previously only undertaken the odd easy ascent in Scotland and the Lake District, maps were no longer a mystery to me, and I started to find more and more mountains to ascend . . . Wales wasn't just Snowdon and Glyder Fawr, Tryfan and Carnedd Llywelyn! Inevitably there came a time when, being an administrator by training, a decision to do a proper job could no longer be avoided. The result was my own list of the 2000-feet summits of North Wales.

Later, exploring the Snowdonia National Park further, I sat for a while on Drws Bach in the Arans and recall feeling that I was on holiday, I was somewhere that didn't belong to North Wales. Only a short time later, on my way to an Eisteddfod in South Wales, I was amazed to discover 'mountains' in South Wales. There was nothing for it; that list of North Wales mountains was about to be extended to the whole of Wales. For the purposes of this book I have converted (and rounded) my original 2000 feet criterion to 600 metres. It's really quite a daft distinction which no one should take too seriously. My concern is with enjoyable walks, not academic niceties, and a line had to be drawn somewhere, so, with one or two exceptions, 600 metres it is.

Not every line of ascent up a mountain is given, in some

◄ Seen across Llynnau Mymbyr from Capel Curig, the peaks of the Snowdon Horseshoe offer a rewarding challenge.

cases for good reason. Nor, for reasons of space, have I given a route up *every* mountain, and, anyway, I have no wish to destroy all the sense of adventure that these wonderful hills afford. But what is given represents a full and good reflection of all that is splendid among *The Mountains of Wales*.

None of the routes I have described poses technical difficulties in good weather conditions in summer. They are not climbs, in the main they are walks, though a few require the ability to scramble – the Bristly Ridge, Tryfan, the Snowdon Horseshoe, but not much more. If there are problems of this kind, I have mentioned them in the text. Most of the walks can also be completed in good winter conditions, though crampons may be required sometimes for security and confidence. But in winter, with snow on the ground, an ice-axe is always essential, as is the knowledge to use it.

When all the hill wandering was done I asked Frances, a relative newcomer to Wales, to give me five highlights of the time we spent there that she would like to relive. All her responses were, of course, subjective, and very much coloured by some excellent weather conditions. She chose: 1. The traverse of Crib Goch – a day of warm sun with bright waves of cloud spilling over Snowdon and Y Lliwedd, and a day on which not for the first time we saw the Brocken Spectre; 2. The ascent of Carnedd Llywelyn from Helyg – for her using crampons for the first time; 3. A superb day across Hay Bluff and Twmpa, at the end of which we spent an hour dangling our feet over the escarpment of Pen Rhos Dirion while buzzards and gliders did battle in the air and wild ponies munched their way placidly across the moorland behind us; 4. The memory of flower-decked hedgerows in the narrow lanes leading on to the Brecon Beacons from the north; and 5. The sheer pleasure of bathing naked in Llyn y Fan Fawr both on the ascent and descent of Ban Brycheiniog and Bannau Sir Gaer. To these I would add an afternoon tea of cream scones and sandwiches at Tan y Pistyll after a day battling through snow on the Berwyn Hills.

If, with the aid of this book, you find pleasurable memories like these, then I will be happy with my work.

Explanatory Notes

Table 1 – set out on pages 15–20 – lists, in order of altitude, all elevations of 600 metres or more, based on a survey of the latest 1:10000 scale Ordnance Survey maps, with a minimum of 30 metres of re-ascent from all directions. It also contains an appendix of elevations of sufficient topographical merit with between 15 and 30 metres of re-ascent. The guide-lines I have followed are those determined by Percy Donald in his *Hills in the Scottish Lowlands, 2000 feet and above*, and contained in the Munros Tables.

The reasons for my use of maps at a scale of 1:10000, which are too large for outdoor use and are sometimes difficult to obtain, are quite simple. The objectives of this book are twofold: firstly, to supply the walker with a wide selection of routes up as many of the Welsh mountains as possible; secondly, and this is where the large scale maps come in, I have tried to make the list of summits contained in Table 1 as accurate and meaningful as possible. Using large scale maps allows me to pinpoint *exactly* (in all but a few difficult instances) where the highest point of the mountain lies – it isn't always the trig point! – and facilitates careful measurement of re-ascent. If you check my calculations with the reality of the ground, you will see that everything is not quite as the commonly used 1:50000 maps suggest. However, having done my calculations for re-ascent and for the map references of summits on the 1:10000 maps, I have then reverted for the rest of this work to using 1:50000 maps like everyone else. Map references of all other features, for example, are from the 1:50000 maps.

This book contains only one simple diagrammatic map.

The vast area to be covered would require an inordinate number of detailed maps to be of any value to the walker. In my opinion there is no substitute for the Ordnance Survey 1:50000 maps which are, after all, essential items for every walker.

Heights Heights are the latest available from the Ordnance Survey and may differ from those on published maps. If there is no height available, the height shown in the Tables is that of the highest contour ring. In these cases the height is followed by the letter c.

Distances and Ascents These are approximate and have been rounded up or down.

Rights of Way. Any reference to paths or other lines of ascent does not imply that a right of way exists.

Names The Ordnance Survey spelling has been used throughout, taken from the 1:10000 maps, which are the most recently published and reflect greater consistency in both spelling and the correct naming of places and mountains. Sometimes this does not agree with names on other maps – 'Ban' Brycheiniog (Section 16), for example, in place of 'Bannau' (which is plural, when in fact there is only one summit). Even so, where a 'new' name appears, the former name (often more widely known) is retained in parentheses – for example, Picws Du (Bannau Sir Gaer), also Section 16. Alternative names are dealt with likewise.

If there is no name on any map, then the name commonly accepted either locally or among hill-walkers has been used. In the absence of anything, the expression 'Unnamed summit' has been adopted, next to which, for purposes of identification, has been given the name of the nearest named summit: if there is no named summit nearby I have resorted to the map reference.

Section names are those commonly in use without regard

to consistency or the niceties of the Welsh language; thus, for example, Carneddau is used instead of Carnedds, but Rhinogs instead of Rhinogydd.

Access to the Mountains of Wales

During the preparation of this book I have walked in every part of Wales. At no time was my presence challenged, though legitimately it could have been on many occasions, as every part of Wales belongs to someone, and unless there is a recognised right of way across land we have no right to be there.

In return for access, let us remember to treat mountain farmland properly. Mountain farms are generally divided into three parts: the lowest, around the farmstead, is used mainly for grazing or the growth of fodder, etc.; the next area is known in Wales as the *ffridd*, and is the area contained by walls and fences; above that is the rough mountain pasture. The uses of all three areas are well explained in Thomas Firbank's book *I Bought a Mountain*. It is important then that we do nothing to alter conditions in these three areas as we find them.

The most common cause of complaint is that gates are left open or walls demolished by people climbing over them. At various points I have laid a route through a gap in a wall, but that's a different thing from clambering over and dislodging drystone walling enclosures which are essential to the sheep farmer's stock management. It's not only a case of animals straying: rams must not be allowed to mix with the ewes until October so that the lambs will be born after the worst rigours of a Welsh mountain winter. If open gates allow them to mix too soon, lambing will occur too early and many lambs will die.

In particularly bad weather, take care that you do not startle groups of ewes and lambs. Many lambs die because their mothers are startled by the sudden appearance of humans, and escape by crossing streams. It is often impossible for the lambs to follow, and so they come to be abandoned. Never attempt to handle a lost new-born lamb, however pathetic and helpless it may look. Leaving human scent on it may drive the mother to abandon the lamb. If you find a lamb, seemingly lost, or injured, report it to the farmer. He can't be all that far away.

Dogs are another form of disaster for the farmer. In the mountains your dog is in an alien environment, and no matter how well controlled and behaved at home, curiosity may well get the better of it in the presence of sheep. Anyway the sheep don't know it's a paragon of all canine virtues. Sheep are instinctively nervous of dogs; if it were not so farmers would not use dogs to round them up. A sheep being chased across the hillside by your dog could suffer an abortion, direct injury or death, or could be forced to escape by jumping on to mountain ledges where it becomes trapped. So, to maintain a peaceful co-existence with the farmers, keep your dog on a lead or long rope – if only to set an example to others.

Not all mountain land is farmland, the Forestry Commission, the Water Authority, the National Trust, and the Nature Conservancy Council all have considerable interests. Generally speaking, the Forestry Commission welcomes the public on foot to all its forests, provided this access does not conflict with the management and protection of the forest. Likewise the other three major concerns are happy to have walkers on their land providing they observe the Country Code and recognise that at certain times of the year – the breeding season, for example – and in some nature reserves and on tenanted farms access may need to be restricted.

Table 1
The 600-metre mountains of Wales
arranged in order of altitude

with a minimum of 30 metres of re-ascent from all directions

	HEIGHT (m)		SECTION	RANGE
1	1085	Yr Wyddfa (Snowdon)	1	Snowdon
2	1065	Crib y Ddysgl (Carnedd Ugain)	1	Snowdon
3	1064	Carnedd Llywelyn	3	Carneddau
4	1044	Carnedd Dafydd	3	Carneddau
5	999	Glyder Fawr	2	Glyders
6	990	Glyder Fach	2	Glyders
7	978	Pen yr Ole Wen	3	Carneddau
8	976	Foel Grach	3	Carneddau
9	962	Yr Elen	3	Carneddau
10	947	Y Garn	2	Glyders
11	942	Foel Fras	3	Carneddau
12	926	Garnedd Uchaf	3	Carneddau
13	923	Elidir Fawr	2	Glyders
14	923	Crib Goch	1	Snowdon
15	915	Tryfan	2	Glyders
16	905	Aran Fawddwy	9	Arans
17	898	Y Lliwedd	1	Snowdon
18	893	Pen y Gadair (Cader Idris)	8	Cader Idris
19	886	Pen y Fan	15	Brecon Beacons
20	885	Aran Benllyn	9	Arans
21	873	Corn Du	15	Brecon Beacons
22	872	Moel Siabod	5	Siabod
23	872	Erw y Ddafad Ddu	9	Arans
24	863	Mynydd Moel	8	Cader Idris
25	854	Arenig Fawr	7	Arenigs
26	849	Llwytmor	3	Carneddau
27	833	Pen yr Helgi Du	3	Carneddau
28	831	Foel Goch	2	Glyders
29	827	Moel Sych	10	Berwyn Hills
30	827	Cadair Berwyn	10	Berwyn Hills
31	822	Carnedd y Filiast	2	Glyders
32	813	Mynydd Perfedd	2	Glyders
33	813	Cyfrwy	8	Cader Idris
34	810	Waun Fach	14	Black Mountains

35	807	Bera Bach	3	Carneddau
36	805	Nameless Peak	2	Glyders
37	802	Ban Brycheiniog	16	Mynydd Du
38	800	Pen y Gadair Fawr	14	Black Mountains
39	799	Pen Llithrig y Wrach	3	Carneddau
40	795	Cribyn	15	Brecon Beacons
41	794	Bera Mawr	3	Carneddau
42	791	Mynydd Pencoed	8	Cader Idris
43	785	Cadair Bronwen	10	Berwyn Hills
44	783	Moel Hebog	4	Hebog
45	780	Glasgwm	9	Arans
46	770	Moelwyn Mawr	5	Moelwyns
47	770	Drum	3	Carneddau
48	769	Waun Rydd	15	Brecon Beacons
49	763	Gallt yr Ogof	2	Glyders
50	761	Fan Hir	16	Mynydd Du
51	758	Drosgl	3	Carneddau
52	756	Y Llethr	6	Rhinogs
53	754	Gwaun Cerrig Llwydion	15	Brecon Beacons
54	752	Pen Pumlumon Fawr	11	Plynlimon
55	751	Moel Llyfnant	7	Arenigs
56	750	Diffwys	6	Rhinogs
57	749	Picws Du (Bannau Sir Gaer)	16	Mynydd Du
58	747	Yr Aran	1	Snowdon
59	742	Tomle	10	Berwyn Hills
60	741	Pen Pumlumon Arwystli	11	Plynlimon
61	734	Craig Cwm Silyn	4	Nantlle
62	734	Fan Fawr	16	Fforest Fawr
63	734	Rhobell Fawr	7	Arenigs
64	730	Unnamed summit (Fan y Big)	15	Brecon Beacons
65	727	Unnamed summit (Pumlumon Fawr)	11	Plynlimon
66	726	Moel Eilio	1	Eilio
67	725	Fan Gihirych	16	Fforest Fawr
68	720	Rhinog Fawr	6	Rhinogs
69	719	Fan y Big	15	Brecon Beacons
70	719	Pen Allt Mawr	14	Black Mountains
71	713	Pen Rhos Dirion	14	Black Mountains
72	712	Rhinog Fach	6	Rhinogs
73	710	Moelwyn Bach	5	Moelwyns
74	709	Trum y Ddysgl	4	Nantlle
75	701	Garnedd Goch	4	Nantlle
76	701	Pen Cerrig Calch	14	Black Mountains

77	698	Mynydd Mawr	4	Nantlle
78	698	Allt Fawr	5	Moelwyns
79	695	Mynydd Drws y Coed	4	Nantlle
80	691	Foel Wen	10	Berwyn Hills
81	690	Twmpa	14	Black Mountains
82	689	Cnicht	5	Moelwyns
83	689	Arenig Fach	7	Arenigs
84	689	Foel Hafod Fynydd	9	Arans
85	685	Pen y Bryn Fforchog	9	Arans
86	685	Gwaun y Llwyni	9	Arans
87	684	Y Garn	11	Plynlimon
88	683	Gau Craig	8	Cader Idris
89	681	Mynydd Tarw	10	Berwyn Hills
90	679	Chwarel y Fan	14	Black Mountains
91	679	Godor	10	Berwyn Hills
92	678	Creigiau Gleision	3	Carneddau
93	677	Hay Bluff (Pen y Beacon)	14	Black Mountains
94	676	Moel Druman	5	Moelwyns
95	674	Maesglasau	8	Dovey
96	674	Moel Cynghorion	1	Eilio
97	672	Ysgafell Wen	5	Moelwyns
98	671	Esgeiriau Gwynion	9	Arans
99	670	Waun Oer	8	Dovey
100	669	Carnedd y Filiast	7	Arenigs
101	669	Unnamed summit (Ysgafell Wen)	5	Moelwyns
102	668	Fan Fraith	16	Fforest Fawr
103	668	Pumlumon Fach	11	Plynlimon
104	667	Cyrniau Nod	10	Berwyn Hills
105	667	Tarren y Gesail	8	Tarren Hills
106	664	Unnamed summit (Pumlumon Fach)	11	Plynlimon
107	663	Fan Nedd	16	Fforest Fawr
108	663	Mynydd Llysiau	14	Black Mountains
109	662	Dduallt	7	Arenigs
110	661	Tyrau Mawr	8	Cader Idris
111	661	Manod Mawr	5	Moelwyns
112	660	Great Rhos	12	Radnor Forest
113	659	Cribin Fawr	8	Dovey
114	658	Pen Twyn Mawr	14	Black Mountains
115	658	Unnamed summit (Manod Mawr)	5	Moelwyns
116	655	Moel yr Ogof	4	Hebog
117	655	Post Gwyn	10	Berwyn Hills

118	654	Allt Lwyd	15	Brecon Beacons
119	653	Mynydd Tal y Mignedd	4	Nantlle
120	650	Black Mixen	12	Radnor Forest
121	648	Foel Cwm Sian Llwyd	10	Berwyn Hills
122	648	Moel yr Hydd	5	Moelwyns
123	646	Pen Twyn Glas	14	Black Mountains
124	646	Pen y Boncyn Trefeilw	10	Berwyn Hills
125	643	Carnedd Llechwedd Llyfn	7	Arenigs
126	641	Drygarn Fawr	13	Elan Valley
127	640c	Unnamed summit		
		(Black Mixen)	12	Radnor Forest
128	638	Moel Lefn	4	Hebog
129	635	Garreg Las (Twyn Swnd)	16	Mynydd Du
130	634	Tarrenhendre	8	Tarren Hills
131	634	Unnamed summit		
		(Creigiau Gleision)	3	Carneddau
132	633	Y Garn	4	Nantlle
133	632	Fan Llia	16	Fforest Fawr
134	630	Moel Fferna	10	Berwyn Hills
135	630	Stac Rhos	10	Berwyn Hills
136	629	Fan Frynych	14	Fforest Fawr
137	629	Y Garn	6	Rhinogs
138	629	Unnamed summit (Craig		
		Cerrig Gleisiad)	16	Fforest Fawr
139	629	Foel Gron	1	Eilio
140	626	Foel y Geifr	10	Berwyn Hills
141	625	Moel y Cerrig Duon	10	Berwyn Hills
142	623	Moel Ysgafarnogod	6	Rhinogs
143	623	Pen y Castell	3	Carneddau
144	623	Moel Penamnen	5	Moelwyns
145	622	Craig y Llyn	8	Cader Idris
146	621	Unnamed summit		
		(089369)	10	Berwyn Hills
147	620	Pumlumon Cwmbiga	11	Plynlimon
148	619	Gallt yr Wenallt	1	Snowdon
149	619	Y Gyrn	15	Brecon Beacons
150	619	Foel Boeth	7	Arenigs
151	619	Garreg Lwyd		
		(Moel Gornach)	14	Mynydd Du
152	617	Cefn yr Ystrad	15	Brecon Beacons
153	617	Fan Dringarth	16	Fforest Fawr
154	615	Cefn Gwyntog	10	Berwyn Hills
155	614	Llechwedd Du	9	Arans
156	613	Gorllwyn	13	Elan Valley
157	612	Trum y Gwrgedd	10	Berwyn Hills

158	611	Foel Goch	7	Arenigs
159	610	Pen yr Allt Uchaf	9	Arans
160	610	Tal y Fan	3	Carneddau
161	610	Bache Hill	12	Radnor Forest
162	610	Foel Goch	10	Berwyn Hills
163	610	Pen y Garn (Bryn Garw)	13	Ystwyth Valley
164	609	Unnamed summit (Bwlch Moch)	1	Snowdon
165	609	Mynydd Troed	14	Black Mountains
166	609	Mynydd Craig Goch	4	Nantlle
167	608	Glan Hafon	10	Berwyn Hills
168	607	Moel Meirch	5	Moelwyns
169	606	Unnamed summit (Moel y Cerrig Duon)	10	Berwyn Hills
170	605	Foel Goch	1	Eilio
171	604	Mynydd Ceiswyn	8	Dovey
172	604	Mynydd Dolgoed	8	Dovey
173	604	Y Gamriw	13	Elan Valley
174	603	Foel Lwyd	3	Carneddau
175	603	Fan Bwlch Chwyth	16	Fforest Fawr
176	602	Y Gribin	9	Arans
177	602	Foel Fraith	16	Mynydd Du
178	600c	Drum yr Eira	13	Elan Valley
179	600	Unnamed summit	17	Rhondda

ADDENDUM

The Black Mountains (Section 14) also contain further summits which straddle the border. They are included here to complete the list of Section 14 summits: Black Hill is wholly in England, the remaining three have their highest points virtually on the border with England.

180	703	Black Mountain	14	Black Mountains
181	640	Black Hill	14	Black Mountains
182	637	Black Daren	14	Black Mountains
183	616	North Daren	14	Black Mountains

NOTES:

1. Where the expression 'Unnamed summit' has been used, it is followed in parentheses by the name of the next nearest, named mountain or other positively identifiable feature.

2. Other names in parentheses are alternative names for the summits.

Other named summits of over 600 metres, with less than 15 metres of re-ascent or which are of little topographical merit.

	MAP REFERENCE	HEIGHT (m)	SECTION	RANGE	1:50 000 OS MAP
Castell y Gwynt★	654582	972	2	Glyders	115
Garnedd Fach★	658626	960c	3	Carneddau	115
Twr y Fan Foel★	824221	802	16	Mynydd Du	160
Elidir Fach	603613	795	2	Glyders	115
Fan Foel	822223	781	16	Mynydd Du	160
Pen y Manllwyn	213309	775	14	Black Mountains	161
Drws Bach	863213	770c	9	Arans	124/125
Dyrysgol	872213	745	9	Arans	124/125
Llechog	605567	718	1	Snowdon	115
Allt Maenderyn★	605528	704	1	Snowdon	115
Pen Trumau	204293	703	14	Black Mountains	161
Twyn Tal-y-cefn	221326	702	14	Black Mountains	161
Cefn Cwm Llwch	017229	701	15	Brecon Beacons	160
Pen Tyrau	837383	697	7	Arenigs	124/125
Craig Ysgafn	660443	689	5	Moelwyns	124
Carnedd y Ddelw	708715	688	3	Carneddau	115
Craig y Fan Ddu	052188	683	15	Brecon Beacons	160
Pencerrigtewion	800881	680c	11	Plynlimon	135
Y Dâs	201328	680	14	Black Mountains	161
Carreg y Diocyn	831363	673	7	Arenigs	124/125
Crib y Rhiw	661250	670c	6	Rhinogs	124
Foel Rhudd	896239	659	9	Arans	124/125
Y Groes Fagl★	988290	659	10	Berwyn Hills	125
Pen Gloch-y-pibwr	202232	657	14	Black Mountains	161
Carnedd y Ci	062341	648	10	Berwyn Hills	125
Gyrn Wigau	654675	643	3	Carneddau	115
Twyn Mwyalchod	022176	642	15	Brecon Beacons	160
Bryn Cras	817895	635	11	Plynlimon	135
Craig Lwyn★	731609	623	3	Carneddau	115
Rhos	124323	619	10	Berwyn Hills	125
Carnedd Lwyd★	683135	616	8	Cader Idris	124
Foel Penolau	661348	614	6	Rhinogs	124
Trum y Sarn★	991302	614	10	Berwyn Hills	125
Pen y Cerrig Duon★	953281	611	10	Berwyn Hills	125
Craig Wen	597509	608	1	Snowdon	115
Bâl Mawr	267271	607	14	Black Mountains	161
Waun Goch★	875202	605	9	Arans	124/125
Moel Ffenigl★	873260	603	9	Arans	124/125
Moel Pearce★	063356	601	10	Berwyn Hills	125
Foel Boethwel★	651477	600c	5	Moelwyns	115

★ Denotes that the summit is not named on the 1:50 000 map.

Section 1 – Snowdon and Eilio

	MAP REFERENCE	HEIGHT (m)	1:50000 OS MAP
Snowdon			
Yr Wyddfa (Snowdon)	609544	1085	115
Crib y Ddysgl			
(Carnedd Ugain)	611552	1066	115
Crib Goch	624552	923	115
Y Lliwedd	622533	898	115
Yr Aran	604515	747	115
Gallt yr Wenallt	642533	619	115
Unnamed summit			
(Bwlch Moch)	635552	609	115
Eilio			
Moel Eilio	556577	726	115
Moel Cynghorion	586564	674	115
Foel Gron	560569	629	115
Foel Goch	571563	605	115

ROUTES
1.1   The Llanberis Path
1.2   The Pig Track
1.3   The Miners' Track
1.4   The Watkin Path
1.5   The Rhyd Ddu Path
1.6   The Snowdon Ranger Path
1.7   Yr Aran
1.8   Crib Goch and Crib y Ddysgl from Pen y Pass
1.9   Y Lliwedd from Pen y Pass
1.10 Gallt yr Wenallt from Nantgwynant
1.11 The Snowdon Horseshoe
1.12 The Figure of Eight
1.13 The Moel Eilio range from Llanberis

The popularity of Snowdon and its outlying mountains has scarcely abated since the first recorded ascent, by a botanist, Thomas Johnson, in 1639. And though all the early ascents were by scientists of one kind or another, by the time George Borrow appeared on the scene to quote

Welsh poetry from Snowdon's summit, in the middle of the nineteenth century, he and his companion were "far from being the only visitors to the hill . . . groups of people, or single individuals, might be seen going up or descending the path as far as the eye could reach."

In 1857 an anonymous writer, commenting on the large number of tourists to North Wales that year, said: "Snowdon is ascended by everyone because it is the highest top; no one seems to ascend the other mountains but the shepherds of the country. Snowdon is the Righi of Wales, with a trifle worse inn at the top." More recently it was estimated in 1924 that approaching 60 000 people made the ascent each year; sixty or more years on the figure is approaching half a million.

What makes it so popular, apart from being the highest and accessible even by railway, is that it has something for everyone. There are easy ways and hard ways to its summit; there are surrounding mountains equally majestic over which to extend one's day; it is virtually encircled by good roads, and it has a flora and fauna to rival many other parts of Wales. In the words of Sir Thomas Noon Talfourd, who compared it with Cader Idris, Helvellyn and Ben Nevis, it "forms . . . the noblest aggregate, because, except on the side opposite Caernarvon, its upper portion is all mighty frame-work, a top uplifted on vast buttresses, disdaining the round lumpish earth, spreading out skeleton arms towards heaven, and embracing on each side huge hollows, made more awful by the red tints of the copper ore which deepens among its shadows, and gleams through the scanty herbage of its loveliest pathways".

Much overshadowed by the mountains of the Snowdon group, those of the Moel Eilio range, lying near to Llanberis, have the advantage of solitude which on a fine day should not be undervalued. This small group of four rounded, grassy hills is a delight to walk, and presents splendid views in particular of Mynydd Mawr across Llyn Cwellyn and the Nantlle ridge, and of the dark cliffs of Clogwyn Du'r Arddu.

▲ *Sunlight catches the ruins of mine buildings beneath the towering north-east face of Snowdon. It was on this face that members of the 1953 Everest expedition practised the techniques which were later to take them to success.*

The reconstructed causeway across Llyn Llydaw now makes the ascent of ▲ *the Miners' Track much easier. Beyond rises the east ridge of Crib Goch.*

Route 1.1 The Llanberis Path The Reverend Bingley, a noted traveller in North Wales during the nineteenth century, tried seven different routes to and from the summit of Snowdon and declared that the way up from Llanberis "is by far the most easy and agreeable, being less steep, less rocky, and less dangerous than any of the others". What he did not say was that it is also the longest, being about 8 kilometres (5 miles), and that it conveys no great sense of feeling for the highest mountain in England and Wales until very near the end of the journey. It does however offer good views of the Moel Eilio range and of the formidable rock-climbing cliff, Clogwyn Du'r Arddu, the scene of the sport's rapid development at the highest standards during the 1960s.

The ascent, which passes through Cwm Brwynog, now climbs in company with the Snowdon Mountain Railway, a tourist contraption introduced in 1896, the only useful function of which seems to be to cart hundreds of visitors to the summit of a mountain they might never otherwise climb. It makes one wonder what we are coming to, especially since as long ago as 1857 writers were saying that "in favourable weather, it is really nothing more than what any person, who has good health, and is accustomed to regular moderate exercise, may without fear or hesitation undertake" (Black's *Picturesque Guide to North Wales*, 1857). The guide goes on to add that, "The indispensable requisites are suitable garments, an early morning start, an experienced guide, some slight provisions, a horn or flask for water, and a resolute abstinence from stimulating beverages, or at least the most scrupulous moderation in the use of them."

Walkers who wish to make the full ascent from Llanberis should start along the road opposite the Royal Victoria Hotel which, after it crosses a cattle grid, climbs steeply through twists and turns (and a gate) for just under one kilometre (about three-quarters of a mile) to a signposted track heading left. At this point the metalled roadway continues ahead to Hafodty Newydd, passing after only a few metres a small area on the left where walkers wishing to omit the initial steep start may park their cars.

The signposted track has in recent years been improved to some extent under a Snowdon Management Scheme, and is now so clear as to be visible even at night without the aid of a torch! It does however tackle the mountain very gently and poses no navigational difficulties until, a short while after the Half-way House refreshment hut, at a fork in the path, the track ascends left to Clogwyn Station where it passes under the railway track. During this short section of the ascent the cliffs of Clogwyn Du'r Arddu become more and more impressive, and on a long summer day a diversion to them will at the very least induce neck ache from gazing acutely upwards at what to non-rock climbers are severely daunting rock walls.

From Clogwyn Station the path ascends the lower

shoulder of Crib y Ddysgl. This is a smooth convex slope which in winter conditions is lethal without at the very least an ice-axe and preferably also crampons. The severity of this section when it is under snow and ice should not be underestimated, nor should walkers be tempted to follow the line of the railway, which simply fills in with snow and presents an equally difficult problem.

Once the shoulder of Crib y Ddysgl has been attained there is a short level walk to a large cairn and then a finger of rock (on the left) which marks the start of the descent into Cwm Dyli and to the Pig Track. The view from here is particularly impressive, east across the upper reaches of Cwm Dyli to the sharp profiles of Crib Goch and Y Lliwedd with Moel Siabod and the Glyders forming a backdrop, and west to the beautiful Nantlle valley hemmed in by the hills of the Nantlle ridge and Mynydd Mawr.

It is now only a few minutes to the summit of Snowdon, walkers customarily taking to the railway track, though a high level route keeping to the rim of upper Cwm Dyli is much more rewarding.

DISTANCE: 8 kilometres (5 miles)
ASCENT: 980 metres (3200 feet)

On the descent care is needed in mist to locate the large cairn just beyond the finger of rock since it marks the start of the path across the shoulder of Crib y Ddysgl. A diversion to this second highest summit from this point is worthwhile on a clear day, giving a superb view of the pyramidal form of Snowdon and the north-east facing cliffs on which climbers heading for the Himalayas have practised their trade.

As an aside it is interesting to note that the current record for the ascent and descent of Snowdon from Llanberis is held by Fausto Bonzi of Italy who in 1984 reduced the previous best to 1 hour 3 minutes and 46 seconds!

Route 1.2 The Pig Track Contrary to a once-popular

belief that the *Pyg* Track takes its name from the initials of the nearby Pen y Gwryd Hotel (the haunt of Everest climbers in years gone by), it is in fact named from the high-level pass, Bwlch y Moch, *Pass of the Pigs*, immediately below the steep ascent to Crib Goch.

The route starts at the top of the Pass of Llanberis, at Pen y Pass, where there is a Youth Hostel, a café, and a never-quite-large-enough car park making a significantly larger charge for parking than the 'shilling' demanded up to the mid-1970s by a man sheltering in a long-since-demolished wooden hut. Walkers who dislike paying parking fees will find that a free Sherpa bus service operates during summer months from Nant Peris where there is a free car park. Unfortunately the Pen y Pass car parking charge seems to continue long after the summer bus service has ended!

Leave the car park through the higher of the two parking areas and pass through a hole in a wall leading to a conspicuous track which has seen improvement in recent years. The track continues by a series of rocky steps beneath the long ridge leading to the unnamed summit (164) just above Bwlch y Moch. This ridge, which can be gained quite easily after the initial steepness of the Pig Track, is by far a more rewarding way to start the ascent.

At Bwlch y Moch the path forks, right, to ascend the steep rocky slopes of Crib Goch, and, left (the Pig Track), actually descending for a short while, to begin an airy traverse of Crib Goch's lower slopes. Llyn Llydaw and its causeway are especially prominent below, and across the lake rise the towering vertical cliffs of Y Lliwedd, rather neglected now by the modern rock climber.

The track is clear throughout its length as it cavorts with minor outcrops, and passes beneath the broken cliffs of Crib y Ddysgl where it joins the Miners' Track ascending from the left. The whole of Cwm Dyli is laid out on the left, and gives photographers ample opportunity to expend film. The final escape from Cwm Dyli, by the well-known zig-zags, has now been reduced to a flight of rock steps as part of the scheme to 'improve' the Snowdon area. True, this section is difficult in winter conditions and requires great care, but it all seems too easy now, and makes me wonder when cable cars will appear!

The top of the zig-zags is now marked by a large finger of rock, and from it there is only a short walk to the summit either along the railway track or by climbing high along the upper rim of Cwm Dyli.

DISTANCE: 4.5 kilometres (2.8 miles)

ASCENT: 730 metres (2400 feet)

Route 1.3 The Miners' Track This is undoubtedly the most popular way up Snowdon, being by a well-graded track once used to bring down copper from the mines of Cwm Dyli. It starts from the car park at Pen y Pass (see Route 1.2 for details) and heads initially in a southerly direction with the long and steep drop to Nantgwynant on the left.

The track soon passes the first of three lakes, Llyn Teyrn, *Lake of the Ruler*, occupying a shallow hollow scooped out by a glacier, and thought to be so named because a local princeling had the sole right to net fish there. On a still day the lake faithfully mirrors the image of Y Lliwedd seen across its waters. On its shores are the ruins of barracks once used by miners working in the copper mines higher in the cwm. Local legend has it that these ruins were occupied by miners from Brittany, who fled at the outbreak of the Napoleonic Wars at the beginning of the nineteenth century; but it is more probable that they were built in the mid-1850s.

Further along the track a corner is turned to reveal the largest lake, Llyn Llydaw, *Brittany Lake*, with the cone of Snowdon seeming to rise vertically from its far end, though there is yet another, hidden, lake to pass first. Llyn Llydaw is divided by a causeway constructed during the last century, once much lower than the present-day causeway and given to frequent flooding, necessitating a circuit of the north-eastern end of the lake to regain the path. The former uneven surface of the causeway made judging the depth of flooding a hit-and-miss task and more than once I have missed a thigh-depth assessment by well over a foot . . . that lake certainly reached places no other lake could reach, with chilling effect!

Once across the causeway, Crib Goch towering on the right, the track circles part of the lake to pass some ruined buildings which were once mills where copper ore was crushed. The mines were never very productive, and although they were supplied with new machinery in 1915 they closed down the following year. Beyond the mills the track climbs steadily to the final lake, Glaslyn. This upper lake, its water tinted remarkably by copper ore, was once named Llyn y Ffynnon Las, *Lake of the Green Fountain*, and is, so legend tells us, inhabited by a monster, an *afangc*, which once lived in a pool near Betws y Coed, causing frequent havoc among the local population. It was moved to Glaslyn by a team of oxen, one of which under severe strain lost an eye at Gwaun Lygad yr Ych, *Field of the Ox's Eye*, on the slopes of Moel Siabod, by which way it came.

From Glaslyn the Miners' Track, which here effectively ends its original purpose, climbs steeply to join the Pig Track (Route 1.2), and escapes from Cwm Dyli by a short series of zig-zags.

DISTANCE: 4.5 kilometres (2.8 miles)
ASCENT: 730 metres (2400 feet)

From the outflow of Glaslyn, which can be crossed easily except after long and heavy rainfall, there is a truly spectacular alternative way to the summit of Snowdon, by the conspicuous descending ridge known as the Cribin (though it is not named on the 1:50 000 map), which leads to Bwlch y Saethau, *Pass of the Arrows*. The ridge is delightfully scrambly and not especially difficult, and it

The view of Crib Goch and the Glyders from the summit of Snowdon. ▶

affords an impressive view down the length of Cwm Dyli with Llyn Llydaw seeming to stretch away interminably. From the top of the ridge join the upper part of the Watkin Path (Route 1.4) to the summit.

Route 1.4 The Watkin Path It was Sir Edward Watkin, a rich and influential railway owner, and one of the original brains behind the idea of a channel tunnel, who constructed the Watkin Path as a donkey track at the end of the nineteenth century. Many years later it is still used as an interesting alternative to more popular routes of ascent to Snowdon, passing as it does through the Cwm y Llan Nature Reserve and into a higher cwm, Tregalan, which is allegedly the scene of one of the ubiquitous King Arthur's many battles.

The path is signposted from the A498, and starts at Bethania Bridge (627506) – near which there is a small car park and toilets – in the beautiful Vale of Gwynant, the scene of many a bloody skirmish in the time of Edward IV between William Earl of Pembroke and the Welsh Lancastrians under Jefan-ap-Robert.

In the lower part of Cwm y Llan stand the ruins of Plas Cwm y Llan once the home of the manager of the slate quarry found a short distance further. The walls of the ruin are pock-marked with rifle fire dating from military training during the Second World War. Further along the path is a large, ice-polished rock into which is set a slate tablet to commemorate the visit in 1892 of W. E. Gladstone, then in his eighty-fourth year and Prime Minister for the fourth time, who addressed the People of Eryri upon Justice to Wales. Later he drove in an open carriage in heavy rain to Aberglaslyn.

The path continues quite clearly beyond Gladstone Rock, and prominent all around are the remains of the South Snowdon Slate Works which commenced operation in 1840, but because of the expense of transporting slates to Porthmadog had to be closed in 1882. Beyond the slate workings the path climbs steadily until it reaches Bwlch

Ciliau, the col between the ridges descending from Snowdon to the north-west and Y Lliwedd to the south-east. There is a large cairn at the bwlch, and from it a path ascends, right, up Y Lliwedd ridge. The Watkin Path however continues left, passing first over Bwlch y Saethau, once itself adorned by a large cairn, Carnedd Arthur, marking one of the legendary sites of the death of King Arthur. From Bwlch y Saethau the path starts to rise abruptly, crossing the southern flank of Snowdon, to arrive at a large finger of rock (an essential marker in descent) at the upper end of Bwlch Main. This section, between Bwlch y Saethau and Bwlch Main, is notoriously loose and very steep, and is a trap for the unwary under winter conditions, when it can become unassailable without ice-axe *and* crampons.

Once at the finger of rock it is a short further ascent, north-east, to the summit.

DISTANCE: 5.5 kilometres (3.4 miles)
ASCENT: 1025 metres (3360 feet)

Route 1.5 The Rhyd Ddu Path Formerly known as the Beddgelert Path, this ascent starts in the village of Rhyd Ddu, at a small car park (571526), where there are also toilets. Begin along a track leading away from the toilets to a gate on the right, which gives access to another track, and soon passes through scattered quarry workings. Beyond the workings the path meanders across relatively low-lying farmland, with the distant cone of Snowdon always in view.

After a little over a kilometre (almost a mile) turn left at the intersection (more noticeable on the map than on the ground) with the route from Beddgelert, and pass through a gate, before starting to ascend the long ridge of Llechog, which now obscures the view of Snowdon. Once the western end of the Llechog ridge is reached Snowdon re-appears across the depression of Cwm Clogwyn, in which repose a number of small lakes. Continue on the path around the rim of the cwm to a steep pull to Bwlch

Main, crossing its west-facing slopes. This section can be intimidating in winter conditions, but can be avoided by keeping to the crest of the ridge. Further on you cross and re-cross the ridge before passing the finger of rock which marks the descent to the Watkin Path. The continuation to Snowdon summit scampers upwards without difficulty.

DISTANCE: 5.5 kilometres (3.4 miles)
ASCENT: 895 metres (2935 feet)

Route 1.6 The Snowdon Ranger Path This route starts near the Youth Hostel (565551), on the shores of Llyn Cwellyn, and is probably the oldest way up Snowdon, being named after a guide, John Morton, who first opened the Snowdon Ranger Inn. It is far less popular with walkers than other routes, despite its proximity to accommodation, and so gives a quieter approach to the moun-

▲ *The Snowdon Horseshoe from near Penygwryd.*

◄ *Y Lliwedd from the summit of Snowdon.*

tain. It is not without its own charms however, having a most impressive view from the top of Clogwyn Du'r Arddu of that amazing cliff formation, and, for most of the ascent, of the wide cwm, Cwm Clogwyn, on the right, dappled with lakes and at the head of which rises Snowdon itself.

The track is easy to follow, starting at the Youth Hostel, where it is signposted, and leads to rising moorland with superb retrospective views of Mynydd Mawr and the Nantlle ridge.

The top of the track, where it meets the Snowdon Mountain Railway, is now marked by a large finger of rock. There is another one a short distance further, at the top of the zig-zag descent into Cwm Dyli, and the two should not be confused: *in descent* the Snowdon Ranger Path is on the *left* of the railway line.

DISTANCE: 5 kilometres (3.1 miles)
ASCENT: 940 metres (3080 feet)

Route 1.7 Yr Aran Because of its isolation from the main range of Snowdon's hills, Yr Aran tends to be neglected, undeservedly so. It is so imposing a peak, particularly seen across Llyn Gwynant or looking down on it in evening sunlight from Bwlch y Saethau in the upper reaches of the Watkin Path, that it is worth undertaking on its own. The approaches are not difficult, and if time permits the continuation to Snowdon, over the minor top, Allt Maenderyn (not named on 1:50000 maps) and across Bwlch Main, is an exhilarating walk. In any event the view towards Snowdon, across Cwm Tregalan, is most imposing.

From Nantgwynant, start at Bethania Bridge (627506) and follow the Watkin Path (Route 1.4) to just before the ruins of Plas Cwm y Llan. Here follow a grassy track on the left rising through mine workings to gain the crest of Yr Aran's east ridge, following a stone wall towards the summit.

DISTANCE: 3 kilometres (1.9 miles)
ASCENT: 685 metres (2250 feet)

From Rhyd Ddu, follow the Rhyd Ddu Path (Route 1.5) to the left turn where that route starts to head for Llechog. Continue straight on instead along a track leading to a disused quarry north-west of Yr Aran, and ascend to the col, Bwlch Cwm y Llan (not named on the 1:50000 maps), from where a rocky ascent, south, leads to the summit.

DISTANCE: 4.5 kilometres (2.8 miles)
ASCENT: 555 metres (1820 feet)

Route 1.8 Crib Goch and Crib y Ddysgl from Pen y Pass The ascent and traverse of Crib Goch is one of the finest ridge walks (though 'walk' is hardly the right word) in the whole of Wales, and compares favourably with similar walks in Scotland, wanting only a little more length to make it a vastly different undertaking. The continuation to Crib y Ddysgl, second only in height to Snowdon itself, does however add more in the way of scrambling, but is not so spectacular as the crest of Crib Goch.

Take the Pig Track (Route 1.2) to Bwlch Moch, where the track forks, left and slightly downhill, for the Pig Track, and, right and definitely uphill, to the broad rock face of Crib Goch. This ascent is so popular that there is little need to describe the route in detail; in fact the physical configuration of the rock outcrops is such that a description would be difficult to follow. The route however is not confusing, and the way marked by thousands of boots. At half height there is a short rock wall which may appear intimidating, more so in descent, but which has ample hand holds to facilitate a scrambly passage to easier ground above.

Contrary to popular belief the actual summit of the mountain is not at the eastern end, but rather nearer to the middle of the ridge, and is marked by a small cairn placed on the very edge of the steep drop into Cwm Glas to the north. Walkers with a good head for heights will find the pleasure of the crossing enhanced by keeping to the very crest all the way, especially when, at the western end, the pinnacles are encountered. More timid walkers, while in no way being discouraged from tackling Crib Goch, except in winter conditions – when it is a major undertaking for everyone – will find the going easier by dropping down slightly from the crest, on the side falling to Cwm Dyli and Llyn Llydaw, and avoiding the pinnacles altogether on the same side.

DISTANCE: 2.5 kilometres (1.6 miles)
ASCENT: 570 metres (1870 feet)

The continuation to Crib y Ddysgl is much less difficult than tackling Crib Goch. A short descent from the pinnacles of Crib Goch leads to a narrow ridge with a minor bump in the middle, and then to a more grassy section before it finally comes up against a shattered rock wall. Most walkers at this point tend to go left a little, and scramble through the rocks, but there is a satisfactory alternative directly ahead, up a short and narrow rock gully from the top of which it is possible to keep nearer to the crest of the ridge with correspondingly better views to the left and right. A short distance further on the ridge narrows abruptly affording a scrambly route along its crest, or a safer option on the north side. Both ways have been boot-marked, and lead without difficulty to the trig point on the summit.

DISTANCE: (from Crib Goch) 1.5 kilometres (1 mile)
ASCENT: 210 metres (690 feet)

Route 1.9 Y Lliwedd from Pen y Pass With their back always to the sun, the dark, north-facing cliffs of Y Lliwedd seem to frown on the vast hollow of Cwm Dyli and its lakes. But early on a summer's morning, or late in the evening, when the light catches these imposing cliffs obliquely they take on a different countenance for a while, pleasing and majestic, and at once inviting and intimidating. There was a time when hard-rock men frequented

Llyn Llydaw, Brittany Lake, *and Snowdon, with Y Gribin ridge outlined by shadow.*

these cliffs with regularity, but not so to the same extent now, leaving them to favour instead playgrounds that do not require quite so much travelling.

For the walker Y Lliwedd is an easy summit to reach, though not without effort. From Pen y Pass take the Miners' Track (Route 1.3) as far as Llyn Llydaw where, on the left, a small green building – a valve house for the Cwm Dyli Power Station, which was opened in 1906 – is encountered. At this point take the track to the valve house, and then continue past it on a rough track heading towards Y Lliwedd. The track rises steeply, and is quite broken in places, making it potentially dangerous in winter conditions. It emerges finally at a large cairn on the col between Y Lliwedd Bach, a small outlier of Y Lliwedd, and Gallt yr Wenallt. Here the track to Y Lliwedd goes right, and ascends to Y Lliwedd Bach before climbing more steeply up a broken, rocky path to the twin summits of Y Lliwedd.

Y Gribin ridge, ascended from the outflow of Glaslyn, is well seen here, and provides excellent scrambling.

Arguments constantly rage as to which of the two summits is the higher, each appearing lower than the other. Modern survey techniques settle the issue; Y Lliwedd West is 898 metres, Y Lliwedd East 893 metres, though seeing may not be believing!

The summits, either of them, have a tremendous feeling of height, being far enough away from Snowdon not to feel too dominated by it, and give an excellent view of the massive amphitheatre of Cwm Dyli, with Crib y Ddysgl appearing as the elongated ridge that it is – something that is not always apparent as you trudge up it.

DISTANCE: 4.5 kilometres (2.8 miles)
ASCENT: 540 metres (1770 feet)

Route 1.10 Gallt yr Wenallt from Nantgwynant The quickest and easiest way to Gallt yr Wenallt is probably by the Miners' Track and then to the col below Y Lliwedd Bach described in Route 1.9, from where a left turn leads across undulating ground to the summit cairn. Strong walkers, however, may well leave the Miners' Track much sooner, before Llyn Teyrn, and head straight for the summit, though this is a wet, steep, arduous and un-marked way only marginally relieved by taking to the north-east ridge.

From Nantgwynant there are two better alternatives, with the advantage on a good day of having the sun on your back all the way. Start at Bethania Bridge (627506) and, for the first, follow the Watkin Path (Route 1.4) as far as the waterfalls prominently marked on the 1:50 000 map. Here descend to a footbridge across the Afon Cwm y Llan and gain an old miners' track leading across the southern flank of Y Lliwedd to disused workings in Cwm Merch. This is a boggy route now, and requires a diversion from it to cross the Afon Cwm Merch, the stream flowing down the obvious cwm, to better ground. Neither the cwm nor the stream is named on the 1:50 000 map. Once across the stream, however, the long ridge rising above Llyn Gwy-

The start of the Pig Track, with the peak of Crib Goch rising in the distance.

nant can be ascended easily to the summit of Gallt yr Wenallt.

DISTANCE: 3.5 kilometres (2.2 miles)
ASCENT: 560 metres (1840 feet)

For the second alternative leave the Watkin Path much sooner at 626510, where the track forks, by taking the right fork. Once across the Afon Cwm y Llan follow a path on the true left bank of the Afon Cwm Merch, through a small wooded area to gain the long summit ridge a little lower down than on the route described above.

DISTANCE: 3.25 kilometres (2 miles)
ASCENT: 560 metres (1840 feet)

Route 1.11 The Snowdon Horseshoe This route is *the* classic walk of North Wales, and is a must for all strong walkers. I emphasise *strong* because it can be very tiring and requires a long day for most mortals, leaving even experienced walkers feeling jaded towards the end. But for all that, *anyone* who gets round it can feel well pleased with himself, as no doubt he will.

It is usual to do the walk in an anti-clockwise direction, though for no particular reason other than the fact that the descent of Y Lliwedd (or Gallt yr Wenallt, if you do the whole thing) at the end is less difficult with tired legs than the descent of Crib Goch. I have therefore described it in this direction, starting at Pen y Pass.

The Pig Track (Route 1.2) is followed to Bwlch y Moch from where the ascent of Crib Goch and Crib y Ddysgl (described in Route 1.8) is made. Purists will of course want to include the First Nail in the Horseshoe, the unnamed summit above Bwlch y Moch, and so it is recommended that the long ridge leading to this small top should be gained as soon as possible after the initial ascent from Pen y Pass.

The final section of the Crib Goch ridge. Keeping to the crest of the ridge is difficult and dangerous, but there are ample hand and foot holds on its southern side.

From Crib y Ddysgl there is a short descent to join the Llanberis Path and the Snowdon Mountain Railway for the equally short ascent to Snowdon's summit.

There is a temptation to descend from Snowdon straight in the direction of Y Lliwedd, but I would counsel against this. The upper part of this descent is terribly eroded and loose, and it is easy to become confused in mist. Opt instead for a short descent down the Rhyd Ddu Path (south-west from the summit) to the large finger of rock, on the left, which marks the top of the Watkin Path, and descend from here. It is still loose and eroded, and extremely difficult in winter conditions, but it is infinitely better than trying to drop straight down from the top of Snowdon – and I choose my words carefully!

On reaching Bwlch y Saethau, climb left, off the Watkin Path, and keep as near as you comfortably can to the edge of the drop into Cwm Dyli. This is much superior to plodding along the lower path, and goes to exactly the same place. En route you will pass the top of the Cribin, a fine scrambly ridge, descending to the outflow from Glaslyn below. This is better as an ascent than a descent, requiring less concentration and giving more time to admire the views.

From Bwlch y Saethau continue to Bwlch Ciliau, where the Watkin Path departs from Cwm y Llan, and continue ahead, climbing again, to the twin summits of Y Lliwedd – the details of Route 1.9 will settle any argument as to which of Y Lliwedd's summits is the higher. From Y Lliwedd East it is a short descent to Y Lliwedd Bach, and then to a cairn at the top of the descent to Llyn Llydaw. Most walkers take this way down, but again purists will want to continue to the Last Nail, Gallt yr Wenallt. The way, from the col, is by a faint path across undulating ground, and is pleasantly easy underfoot after so much hard ground. From the summit of Gallt yr Wenallt descend due north, if necessary taking a bearing on Llyn Teyrn. It is very steep and slippery at first, being on grass, and later, near the Afon Glaslyn, becomes wet and marshy. Once across the pipeline there is a short, almost cruel, re-ascent to join the Miners' Track. This extension to take in Gallt yr Wenallt is probably one of the reasons for most walkers coming down to Llyn Llydaw from Y Lliwedd, and forgetting about the Last Nail altogether!

DISTANCE: 11.25 kilometres (7 miles)
ASCENT: 1040 metres (3415 feet)

Route 1.12 The Figure of Eight This walk is pure invention, designed to get all of the very best out of Snowdon at one go. Greedy, perhaps, but you can always come back for more.

From Pen y Pass ascend to Crib Goch and Crib y Ddysgl, and continue to the summit of Snowdon. If the café is open, use it; it will be closed by the time you next get here. Descend the Rhyd Ddu Path to Rhyd Ddu village, and walk down the road towards the Snowdon Ranger Youth Hostel and ascend the Snowdon Ranger Path from there, or cutting off a little distance by leaving the road at Bron y Fedw Isaf farm (568546). Once back at Snowdon, resume the Horseshoe to Y Lliwedd and, if you want, Gallt yr Wenallt, arriving back at Pen y Pass very tired and very late.

Needless to say a long day is needed, and lots of stamina.

DISTANCE: 22 kilometres (14 miles)
ASCENT: 1980 metres (6500 feet)

Route 1.13 The Moel Eilio range from Llanberis This fine group of four grassy hills is an excellent alternative to the nearby heights of Snowdon or the Glyders at any time of year, but particularly so when the higher mountains are overpopulated.

Start from the car park next to the Royal Victoria Hotel and leave Llanberis along the road to the Youth Hostel, Ffordd Capel Coch, passing the hostel after about half a kilometre. Continue to a gate across the road, and turn right on to a rough, stony track following the line of a stone wall. After only 150 metres (before a second gate) turn left

▲ *Llyn Teyrn,* Lake of the Ruler, *along the Miners' Track, with the mound of Moel Siabod rising in the distance.*

along a green path to join a stone track climbing easily between walls to a white farmhouse building. The track continues through a gate, and climbs to a stile on the right. Cross the stile and then ascend very steeply, left, along the line of a wall to reach a second stile across a fence. After this initial steepness Moel Eilio's north-east ridge is gained and followed to the summit, on the top of which there is a large round stone shelter.

The continuation along the ridge is not clear because the large and flat top of Moel Eilio precludes onward views. The line of stones near the summit does *not* indicate the correct direction for the ridge walk, which is by a faint path descending south-east, and passing through a hole in a wall. This leads without difficulty to the double-topped

The Moel Eilio group of hills, seen from the summit of Snowdon. The lake ▶
in the centre of the picture is Llyn Ffynnon-y-gwas.

summit of Foel Gron, and to Foel Goch before a final steep descent towards Moel Cynghorion. This part of the route is steeper than any other section of the traverse, and it is not direct. The surest guide is to cross the fence (at a stile) which adorns the summit of Foel Goch, and then to follow it round, right at first, and then down to Bwlch Maes-gwm (not named on the 1:50000 map). The ascent to Moel Cynghorion is straightforward, and a small summit cairn will be found in the middle of a wide plateau.

From the summit of Moel Cynghorion descend its steep northern slopes to Helfa (583574), from where there is an easy return to Llanberis by the metalled roadway to Hafodty Newydd.

The range can be ascended without difficulty from the Snowdon Ranger Youth Hostel near Llyn Cwellyn, by taking the Snowdon Ranger Path (Route 1.6) to the high-level pass just before Clogwyn Du'r Arddu, Bwlch Cwmbrwynog, and then ascending steeply, left, to the summit plateau of Moel Cynghorion before embarking along the ridge. A better choice, however, is to start and finish at Llanberis, giving a more convenient round than from Llyn Cwellyn.

DISTANCE: 12 kilometres (7.5 miles)
ASCENT: 990 metres (3250 feet)

▼ *Yr Aran, seen across the waters of Llyn Gwynant.*

Section 2 – Glyders

	MAP REFERENCE	HEIGHT (m)	1:50000 OS MAP
Glyder Fawr	642579	999	115
Glyder Fach	656583	990	115
Y Garn	631596	947	115
Elidir Fawr	612613	923	115
Tryfan	664594	915	115
Foel Goch	628612	831	115
Carnedd y Filiast	620628	822	115
Mynydd Perfedd	623619	813	115
Nameless Peak	678582	805	115
Gallt yr Ogof	685586	763	115

ROUTES

Black's *Picturesque Guide to North Wales*, published in 1857, comments that "In savage grandeur the Glyder is not surpassed by any scene in Wales". It is still a perfectly valid observation. Anyone travelling from Bangor down the A5 through Nant Ffrancon cannot fail to be awed by the high cwms and towering rock walls of the north Glyder ridge stretching from Carnedd y Filiast to Y Garn, by the eeriness of the Devil's Kitchen, and by the abruptness of the massive wall of Glyder Fach which serves as a dominating end to the long valley.

The name 'Glyder' has confused people for many years as to its meaning, but the generally accepted translation is that it means 'a pile, or heap', after the array of tumbled boulders on the summits.

The mountains, rising at their highest to almost 1000 metres, seem to be bounded on all sides by steep cliffs, and though this impression eases along Nantgwryd, better known perhaps as the Dyffryn valley, the severity resumes on the descent of the Llanberis Pass, along which there is a formidable array of cliffs.

Sadly the northern end of the range has been despoiled, mainly by the extraction of slate both at Llanberis and near Bethesda. More recently, though less noticeably, the mountains have been used for a hydro-electric scheme involving the low lying lake, Llyn Peris, and a high glacial lake, Marchllyn Mawr, both of which now fluctuate considerably in their daily process of providing power.

Route 2.1 The Miners' Track from Ogwen to Pen y Gwryd Herbert Carr writing in *The Mountains of Snowdonia* commented that "the Glyders are true mountain ground, and the wanderer must not look for smooth paths upon their craggy ridges". The Miners' Track, which starts by finding a way through such weaknesses as there are between Ogwen and Pen y Gwryd, is no exception to this. It is a relic of the days when hardy quarrymen crossed these rough and broken mountains every week on the journey from their homes at Bethesda to the mines beneath Snowdon's north face. The complete traverse of the Miners' Track across the Glyders seems less popular than it once was even with present-day hill-walkers, but it

Y Garn, above Ogwen, always looks majestic. A covering of snow ▲
enhances the appearance. Seen here from the north ridge of Tryfan.

Glyder Fach and the Bristly Ridge in stormy light, viewed from the summit ▶
of Tryfan.

serves as a convenient access to many of the ascents described later.

At Ogwen the track has been re-routed around new buildings near the Youth Hostel, but after crossing the river soon joins the long-established and popular route to the Cwm Idwal Nature Reserve. After only a short distance (less than a kilometre) the Cwm Idwal path turns sharply right, leaving the Miners' Track to continue ahead to a path which can be seen climbing beside the falls issuing from Llyn Bochlwyd. The short intervening section is uncertain, often boggy, and the path beside the falls eroded and steep, but the outflow of Llyn Bochlwyd is soon reached, and offers a convenient place to recover one's breath. Llyn Bochlwyd is a beautiful lake, surrounded by imposing cliffs; the Gribin on the right, Tryfan behind and to the left, and the popular rock-climbing cliffs of Glyder Fach directly ahead, while across the lower slopes of the Gribin, resting on folded arms, looms Y Garn. Many a good intention has fallen foul of fair Bochlwyd.

Walkers who do not give in to such blatant temptation should continue by a well-marked path, keeping the lake to the right, and gradually climbing to a patch of boggy ground, just above some small falls, over which in wet conditions there is really no easy way, though a line of stepping stones struggle valiantly to keep their summits above the mire. Once across this ground the going improves, and gradually the low point of the skyline, Bwlch Tryfan with its two stiles, comes into view. The path forks here, before the final section up to the bwlch, the left branch climbing steeply to Tryfan's south ridge. This is not the Miners' Track, which keeps right and weaves a way easily through the broken rocks beneath the bwlch.

Bwlch Tryfan is a high-level pass and is particularly imposing. To the left a wall ascends part of the way up Tryfan's south ridge, while to the right it climbs recklessly to the foot of the Bristly Ridge. Ahead lies an open expanse across the head of Cwm Tryfan, banking sharply upwards on the right to Glyder Fach, and sweeping down left to the Ogwen valley and the A5 Holyhead to London road.

The Miners' Track, traversing above Cwm Tryfan, continues by a clearly defined path that can nevertheless demand caution in winter conditions in one or two places; at such times an ice-axe is essential. Finally the track emerges on a plateau containing, to the left, Llyn Caseg Fraith, *Lake of the Piebald Mare*, with the mound of Nameless Peak rising gently beyond it.

The continuation from the edge of Cwm Tryfan to the start of the descent to Pen y Gwryd is not very clear, but the 1:50000 map shows the line quite accurately, and a compass bearing from this leads one safely across the plateau to a more prominent track descending to the road, joining it near to the Pen y Gwryd Hotel.

This hotel is itself a prominent feature in the developing history of mountaineering in North Wales. Supporting Herbert Carr's assertion that "to minister to our needs among mountains nothing is so necessary as a good inn", the Pen y Gwryd started life in the middle of the nineteenth century as "a wayside cottage" at the junction of the road over the Llanberis Pass with that from Capel Curig to Beddgelert. From then, despite (or perhaps because of) Charles Kingsley's opinion that it was "the divinest pigsty beneath the canopy", the Pen y Gwryd has gone from strength to strength, achieving its greatest glory as a base for some of the equipment tests and team meetings in the campaign to climb Everest, when it was frequented by many of the climbers led to success by John Hunt in 1953. Not long ago it was host to the meet celebrating the twenty-fifth anniversary of the ascent.

DISTANCE: 5 kilometres (3 miles)
ASCENT: 460 metres (1510 feet)

Route 2.2 Tryfan by the north ridge The ascent of Tryfan is unquestionably one of the most exhilarating undertakings in the whole of Wales; it is an ascent that, like the traverse of the Crib Goch ridge, would not be out

The Cannon on the ascent of Tryfan's north ridge.

The summit of Glyder Fach.

The Cantilever on Glyder Fach is exactly as it was when Thomas Pennant ▲
visited it 200 years ago. This enormous slab is estimated to weigh over 70
tons.

Beyond Llyn Bochlwyd, on the ascent of the Miners' Track from Ogwen to ▶
Penygrwyd, rises the Gribin ridge.

of place among the hills of Scotland. Walkers who are competent on rock require little in the way of direction; 'up' is often instruction enough, and such a choice of route, wandering among rock walls and buttresses, will afford an entertaining ascent.

Walkers who are less at home on rock need have no fear, however, that Tryfan is barred to them, though it is probably fair to say that the ascent is unlikely to be accomplished confidently with one's hands in one's pockets.

The most convenient ascent of the north ridge starts from the car park on the A5, just below the popular rock-climbing ground, Milestone Buttress. From the car park a path can be found through a jumble of boulders and across a grassy slope leading through more boulders to a stile over a wall immediately beneath Milestone Buttress itself. Beyond the wall a well-marked path ascends steeply at first across loose and broken ground until it emerges on a heather-covered shoulder. The way up the north ridge then becomes apparent, being by a scree track to start and thereafter marked by countless thousands of feet. The route is eroded in places, and can cause problems in winter conditions, but by following the obvious way, generally up the centre of the ridge, the path eventually arrives at a small, quartz-covered plateau to the right of which stands the finger of rock known as the Cannon, a feature clearly seen from the car park below.

A path, left, at this point leads upwards to another small plateau and a rock wall at the base of which there is a tumble of massive boulders and a finely pointed pinnacle not dissimilar to the Cannon below. The wall may seem impassable, but after negotiating the boulders it affords a not-too-difficult direct ascent to the top of a steep gully. By going left through a small gap, however, just below the wall, a short descent and re-ascent on an obvious path leads round a corner into the gully itself, and a scramble over blocks to the top.

From the top of the gully a short scramble upwards

leads across a more level array of boulders to a short descent to the top of yet another, wider gully following which is a final ascent around the Central Buttress to the two large boulders, Adam and Eve, on the summit. This final section is easily negotiated by traversing right from the top of the gully.

Many years ago the practice evolved of stepping from one summit boulder, Adam, to the other, Eve (though which is which has never been clear), but to do so is obviously a matter of choice. Anyone without a good sense of balance and a head for heights would be advised to allow discretion to be the better part of valour.

The ascent of the north ridge may also be accomplished from the farm, Gwern Gof Uchaf (673604), where there is a small car park. Follow Route 2.4, the Heather Terrace route, until it emerges from the top of the scree gully (by a steep rock wall), and instead of turning left, for the terrace, continue ahead, still climbing a little, until it is possible to ascend to the scree track referred to earlier.

DISTANCE: 1 kilometre (0.6 miles)
ASCENT: 615 metres (2020 feet)

Route 2.3 Tryfan by the south ridge The ascent of Tryfan by the south ridge, particularly by walkers who are not entirely happy scrambling about on rock that can at times feel a little exposed, will prove a far less daunting proposition than that by the north ridge. The ascent from the south is in any event a pleasant and more leisurely way up the mountain.

Route 2.1 describes the Miners' Track from Ogwen to Pen y Gwryd, and this track should be followed from Ogwen, up beside the Bochlwyd falls to Llyn Bochlwyd grandly situated beneath the great cliffs of Glyder Fach, until the two stiles are encountered across the wall at Bwlch Tryfan. It is not necessary to cross the wall, but instead to ascend left (northwards) about 400 metres before the wall along an obvious path over stony ground to the foot of Tryfan's south summit. There are many ways from this point, but as soon as the ground steepens the easiest going will be found away from the wall. Whichever route is chosen, and the ways are now well marked, little difficulty should be encountered.

Used in descent the south ridge is a way with little difficulty providing care is taken to avoid a few sudden drops which are not quite so apparent on the ascent. Most of these can be avoided by travelling (in descent) rather more to the right of the main axis of the mountain.

DISTANCE: 2.5 kilometres (1.6 miles)
ASCENT: 615 metres (2020 feet)

Route 2.4 Tryfan by the Heather Terrace The ascent of Tryfan by the Heather Terrace starts from the farm, Gwern Gof Uchaf (673604), though 'ascent' is an inappropriate word for a route which traverses the steep east face of the mountain, only finally ascending significantly as it nears the south ridge.

Go around the farmhouse and over a stile, followed by a

Castell y Gwynt, Castle of the Winds, *is all that remains of a minor summit. It is not so difficult to cross as may be imagined, but there is an easy way around by a path on the south side (left, in this picture). Beyond, to the left, rises the peak of Snowdon, and, to the right, the castellated summit of Glyder Fawr.*

The summit of Glyder Fach, and Castell y Gwynt, seen from the top of the Gribin ridge.

The highest part of Y Gribin ridge, which rises from Llyn Bochlwyd to Bwlch y Ddwy Glyder.

short path to a second stile. The path continues to the foot of Little Tryfan, a rock-climbing training ground of moderate difficulty, and then, right, across marshy ground, to ascend a wide scree gully which is plainly in view. The gully narrows and becomes very loose at the top where it is dominated by a steep rock wall on the right. From the top of this gully go left, along an obvious path, and wander through numerous boulders amid deep heather and bilberry until the terrace proper starts to rise across the east face. A succession of gullies and intermediate buttresses tower on the right, with the wide expanse, left, of Cwm Tryfan.

At the end of the terrace the track rises, right, and ascends to a stone wall over which there are two stiles. Across the wall it is possible to join the south ridge route and scramble easily to the summit.

DISTANCE: 2.25 kilometres (1.4 miles)
ASCENT: 610 metres (2000 feet)

Route 2.5 Glyder Fach by the Bristly Ridge The ascent of the Bristly Ridge is unquestionably one of the highlights of hill walking in Wales. It is, technically, a rock scrambling route, but on which only the most timid are likely to find anything to test their nerve, and the overall feeling is one of great exhilaration. There are no insurmountable difficulties, and for most of the way the route is enclosed by rock walls which significantly lessen any feeling of exposure.

Route 2.1 – the Miners' Track – is the key to the ascent from Ogwen, this approach being shorter than ascent along the same track from Pen y Gwryd. Follow the Miners' Track past Llyn Bochlwyd and as far as the wall across Bwlch Tryfan, crossing it by one of the stiles. The shelter of the wall is a convenient place to rest before turning right to face, high above, a seemingly impenetrable wall of rock. Nearer to hand a section of broken rock has a number of well-worn paths criss-crossing its surface, some more eroded than others, but by labouring up this tiring section the path finally leads by a short scree slope to the foot of an obvious gully. This is the start of the Bristly Ridge.

From the bottom of the gully the route upwards is well marked, twisting and turning through a maze of rock walls that make it impossible, and unnecessary, to describe the way with any meaningful directions. Only near the top does the route tend to open out, and by then an easy path can be gained which leads to a small plateau at the very top of the ridge. The retrospective view, down to Tryfan, is tremendously impressive, and inspired Thomas Pennant, a noted and reliable traveller of his time, to write just 200 years ago: "In the midst of the vale far below rises a singular mountain *Trevaen*, assuming on this side a pyramidal form, naked and very rugged."

The descent of the Bristly Ridge is every bit as entertaining as the ascent, but walkers looking upwards from Bwlch Tryfan will notice on the left a conspicuous scree slope descending the entire height of the ridge, and this may be used as an alternative descent (or ascent – for those who enjoy boredom and sheer hard work), though it is very loose and needs care in winter conditions.

From the top of the Bristly Ridge it is a short way ahead and slightly left, following a line of cairns, to a prominent jumble of rocks, perched atop of which is the famous Cantilever, an immense balanced block estimated to weigh more than seventy tons. The actual summit of Glyder Fach is nearby, an even greater jumble of boulders and slabby rocks, surprisingly easy to miss in dense mist.

Further ahead lies the summit of Glyder Fawr, the higher of the two Glyders, with the way to it apparently barred by a gnarled array of rocky teeth and turrets known as the Castell y Gwynt, *Castle of the Wind*. This strange configuration is not so difficult to cross as might be imagined, but walkers not wishing to tackle it should follow a clear path descending, left, and around it (in the direction Glyder Fach to Glyder Fawr), and finally climbing again across a shoulder of broken rocks and stones to re-join the path to the castellated summit rocks of the higher mountain.

DISTANCE: (To Glyder Fach only) 2.5 kilometres (1.6 miles)

ASCENT: 690 metres (2265 feet)

Route 2.6 Glyder Fawr/Glyder Fach by Y Gribin Y Gribin is a long ridge descending from a small plateau, Bwlch y Ddwy Glyder, *Pass of the Two Glyders*, near the jagged pinnacles of the Castell y Gwynt. The base of the ridge sprawls around from the Bochlwyd falls to the rock-climbing cliffs of the Gribin Facet overlooking Cwm Idwal, and ascents of the ridge can easily be accomplished from both these extreme ends.

From Ogwen take the path to the gate at the entrance to the Cwm Idwal Nature Reserve, and then bear left to ascend grassy slopes to the left of the cliffs, and so on to the ridge. An easier alternative is to ascend by the Bochlwyd falls (using the Miners' Track – Route 2.1), and from the outflow of Llyn Bochlwyd bear right to gain the ridge.

The lower part of Y Gribin is grassy, but it becomes rocky and more exposed higher up and needs care: halfway is marked by a surprisingly large field, the size of a football pitch, which lies above the popular climbing route, Cneifion Arête. The top of the ridge, when it comes, is marked by a large cairn, and from it, as on the ascent, there is a very impressive view of the crags of Glyder Fach and Castell y Gwynt.

From the cairn Glyder Fach may be reached by crossing (or passing round, by a path on the south side) the Castell y Gwynt. Glyder Fawr, however, lies to the right, beyond the steep drop into Cwm Cneifion. Although there is a path all the way to Glyder Fawr, it lies across rocky ground and is not always clear in misty conditions, but it is cairned for most of the way. Thomas Pennant says of Glyder Fawr: "The elements seem to have warred against this moun-

Twll Du, Black Hole, *is an enormous gash in the upper cliffs of the Devil's Kitchen.* ▶

tain, rains have washed away the soil, lightnings have rent its surface, and the winds make it the constant object of their fury." The battle still goes on 200 years later.

DISTANCE: Glyder Fach 3 kilometres (1.9 miles); Glyder Fawr 3.25 kilometres (2 miles)

ASCENT: Glyder Fach 690 metres (2265 feet); Glyder Fawr 695 metres (2280 feet)

Route 2.7 Glyder Fawr by Cwm Idwal and the Devil's Kitchen The ascent to Glyder Fawr through Cwm Idwal and by way of the Devil's Kitchen is probably the most energetic way to the tops, but it is always impressive, with constantly changing views to distract one's attention from heavy breathing and aching limbs.

The route starts around the new buildings near the Youth Hostel at Ogwen, and follows the well established path into Cwm Idwal, according to Thomas Pennant "a fit place to inspire murderous thoughts, environed with horrible precipices, shading a lake, lodged in its bottom". According to Pennant, "no bird dare fly over its damned water, fatal as that of *Avernus*".

At the gate into the reserve turn left and continue along the shore of Llyn Idwal to the popular rock-climbing ground, the Idwal Slabs, on whose polished and nail-scarred slopes generations of mountaineers have cut their teeth. Beyond the Slabs the path starts to rise in a series of man-made steps to the foot of an immense downfall of boulders beneath the cliffs which flank Twll Du, *Black Hole*, which Pennant describes as a "dreadful aperture". In certain wind conditions this enormous cleft is said to produce weird sounds, and when this coincides with swirling mists, as it all too frequently does, it gives good reason for lending to this area the description, 'Devil's Kitchen'. A number of paths find ways through the boulders, but it is worth making for the very foot of Twll Du, in spite of Pennant's reservations, to appreciate its full grandeur. There is, too, a wealth of vegetation growing in its crevices that will interest the botanist, among them Wood Sorrel, Wood Anemone and the Snowdon Lily, *Lloydia serotina*.

From Twll Du a path ascends, left, beneath the towering cliffs, and leads finally to a lake, Llyn y Cwn, *Lake of the Dogs*, so named from a tradition of hunting in this area. Llyn y Cwn is a pleasant place to relax, and it is wise to do so before tackling the next part of the route.

Immediately before you reach Llyn y Cwn an obvious path, turning to scree higher up, ascends a gully to the left. At first it is confined by rocky outcrops, but degenerates into an open, worn path of loose soil and scree which requires extreme care at all times, especially in descent. In winter conditions this short section, either in ascent or descent, can be dangerous; it is a convex slope on which one slip could precipitate an uncontrolled fall on to the screes below. This section should not be attempted in

Late evening sunlight casts its rays across Llyn Idwal on to the Idwal Slabs.

winter conditions without at least an ice-axe (and the knowledge to use it properly).

Once the steepness of the ascent starts to ease the path is marked by a line of large cairns, and leads without undue difficulty to the castellated summit of Glyder Fawr. The continuation to Glyder Fach starts by a worn path marked by a line of cairns, and though possibly confusing in mist, is generally not difficult to follow.

DISTANCE: 3.5 kilometres (2.2 miles)
ASCENT: 695 metres (2280 feet)

Route 2.8 Glyder Fawr from Pen y Pass This is one of the least popular ways to Glyder Fawr, many walkers no doubt being put off by the formidable array of cliffs which make up the northern side of the Llanberis Pass, though none of these is encountered on the ascent. Yet the route deserves to be more popular for its unusual line, for the views it gives of the Snowdon massif, and, for the moment, for its solitude. It forms part of a high-level way across the Glyders to Capel Curig, a Courtesy Path, organised by the Snowdonia National Park Society, which won a coveted Prince of Wales Award.

Start from the car park at the top of the Llanberis Pass, though anyone not wishing to pay the fee in summer may park free at Nant Peris and travel up and down the pass in a Sherpa bus. Begin over the stile (646556) on the Llanberis side of and close to the Pen y Pass Youth Hostel, and immediately pick up a path marked by small red-paint circles. The path quickly ascends a low ridge, bringing Llyn Cwm y Ffynnon into view on the right, and starts to climb steadily, roughly parallel with the main road below until it reaches the bottom of a broad rocky shoulder falling from the summit of Glyder Fawr. The way up the shoulder is well marked and as it steepens the path zig-zags to ease the gradient. Continue always in a general northerly direction until the summit is reached.

DISTANCE: 3 kilometres (1.9 miles)
ASCENT: 645 metres (2115 feet)

Route 2.9 Glyder Fawr from Gwastadnant This route, as far as Llyn y Cwn, is more often taken as a short cut across the mountains, joining Llanberis with Ogwen, but it can be used by walkers based in or around Llanberis to give access to the northern mountains of the Glyder range as well as to the Glyders themselves.

The route starts along a stony track (signposted) which leaves the A4086 at 614576, next to a camp-site. The track leads in a short distance to a small wooden gate, and then to a path climbing very steeply at first with the Afon Las. As the ground levels, approaching Llyn y Cwn, it tends to become boggy, but is seldom in doubt.

At Llyn y Cwn join Route 2.7 to ascend to Glyder Fawr.
DISTANCE: 3.25 kilometres (2 miles)
ASCENT: 880 metres (2890 feet)

Route 2.10 The ridges of Y Garn Y Garn is a most impressive mountain, the full grandeur of which is best seen from the summit of Tryfan. Its ridges form encircling arms around a wild cwm in which repose two small lakes, known by the singular name, Llyn Clyd – presumably they were once one lake. A silty, connecting neck of land supports this theory. To reach the lakes is well worth the effort, and the two ridges make a satisfactory round trip in themselves.

From Ogwen take a path which ascends behind the new shop and toilet building near the Youth Hostel. This joins the well-established route into the Cwm Idwal Nature Reserve, and at the entrance to the reserve, at the gate, go right across a wooden bridge and follow a clear path around the edge of Llyn Idwal. Walkers intending to ascend by the south-east ridge should cross the stream coming from Llyn Clyd and follow an obvious fishermen's path to the cwm, then bear left and upwards through broken cliffs and rocky outcrops to gain the ridge. The upper edge of the cwm defines the way to the stone shelter on the summit.

The north-east ridge can be reached, again by a stiff

climb, by ascending from Llyn Idwal directly up the broad shoulder until a well-trodden path is gained. The view northwards to Foel Goch, across Cwm Cywion, with Elidir Fawr peering over the intervening ridge, is especially imposing.

The top of the north-east ridge is marked by a collapsed cairn on a small plateau – not to be mistaken for the summit, which lies a short way south and up.

Since the apex of the south-east ridge, where it meets the route from Cwm Clyd, is difficult to locate in mist, it is probably better to ascend by the south-east ridge and descend by the north-east.

DISTANCE: (Round trip) 5 kilometres (3.2 miles)
ASCENT: 645 metres (2115 feet)

Route 2.11 Y Garn to Carnedd y Filiast and Elidir Fawr The ridge forming the westerly boundary of Nant Ffrancon is relatively infrequently visited, though its traverse provides an entertaining walk comparable with anything in and around Ogwen.

From Ogwen, Y Garn should be reached by either of the ridges described in Route 2.10, or by following Route 2.7 through Cwm Idwal to Llyn y Cwn above the Devil's Kitchen. Near Llyn y Cwn a path ascends the rounded slopes of Y Garn's western flank, against which the steep eastern face contrasts sharply.

An alternative ascent from the top of the path out of the Devil's Kitchen and along the edge of the cliffs will lead first to the chasm of Twll Du, *Black Hole*, and then upwards to join Y Garn's south-east ridge.

Beyond Y Garn the ridge can be seen undulating northwards, with the bulk of Elidir Fawr prominent on the left. An easy descent leads to a grassy col above Cwm Cywion (not named on the 1:50 000 map) and the start of a gentle rise, first over a small plateau, and then upwards to the collapsed cairn on the summit of Foel Goch, from where there is an excellent view across Nant Ffrancon to Pen yr Ole Wen and the more distant Carneddau. More descent,

The western prospect of Tryfan seen across the waters of Llyn Idwal.

following the edge of the ridge, leads to Bwlch y Brecan, across which there is what is thought to be an old pack-horse route connecting Nant Ffrancon with Nant Peris.

From Bwlch y Brecan a well-trodden path skirts the insignificant mound of Mynydd Perfedd, and swings west to the rocky top of Elidir Fawr, affording a view down into the cwm containing Marchlyn Mawr, a dammed lake now used as part of the Dinorwic Pumped Storage Scheme.

A return towards Bwlch y Brecan, but keeping left and avoiding unnecessary descent, will lead on to Mynydd Perfedd and then to Carnedd y Filiast, the most northerly summit of the group, from where a descent may be made to Nant Ffrancon by the ridge immediately north-east of the summit. This is heathery, and steep in places, and leads on to the old road through the valley.

DISTANCE: (Round trip from Ogwen): Up to 15 kilometres (9 miles) according to choice of route

ASCENT: Up to 1065 metres (3495 feet)

Alternative descents (also useful in the event of bad weather) may be made by Y Garn's north-east ridge; Foel Goch's south-east ridge; by the old pack-horse route across Bwlch y Brecan, either east or west; and in a south-westerly direction from virtually any point by following the fall of the ground towards Nant Peris, taking care however to avoid minor rock outcrops. Do not attempt to descend Yr Esgair, the north-east ridge of Foel Goch. This is an extremely difficult scramble, and should be avoided.

Route 2.12 Elidir Fawr from Nant Peris The sight of Elidir Fawr from Llanberis is not one for sore eyes. Once named Carnedd Elidir in commemoration of Elidir Mwynfawr, son-in-law of Maelgwm, Prince of Gwynedd,

The easy slopes of the Nameless Peak, with Gallt yr Ogof beyond. On the left lies Llyn Caseg Fraith, Lake of the Piebald Mare.

it is now a mountain that has been ravaged by man's industry, first as a slate quarry, and more recently though less obtrusively for a hydro-electric scheme. For this reason an ascent from Llanberis is virtually impossible and, other possibly than for industrial archaeologists, wholly uninteresting. Just over 3 kilometres (2 miles) down the Llanberis Pass, however, lies the village of Nant Peris from where a more acceptable ascent may be made.

The route starts along a minor road where the Afon Gafr flows under the A4086, about 150 metres from the Vaynol Arms. A short way along the road go sharp left (not ahead, which leads into a farm), and continue for just under a kilometre (about half a mile) until the road ends at an old cottage. This is Fron (605590), a climbers' hut, where there is limited parking, but it is better to park in Nant Peris and to walk the short distance to Fron.

Gallt yr Ogof, from the A5 London to Holyhead road.

Pass through a gate marked by a public footpath sign at the side of the cottage, and go uphill to a stile at the top of the field. Over the stile a green track appears leading to a gate at the top of the next field. From here the road is enclosed for a short distance before giving out on to open hillside and a series of zig-zags which climb to above a stone wall. A clear road now heads to the right (east-northeast), climbing gently with the Afon Dudodyn on the left. In a short while it is necessary to cross the river at a bridge with a single handrail, and then to continue, away from the green track, straight up the grassy hillside to a prominent bump. From this bump continue along a minor grassy ridge, with prominent spoil heaps on the left, to cross a stone wall at a stile.

At this stile it is advisable to head diagonally across the upper slopes of Cwm Dudodyn for the summit of Elidir Fawr. This is infinitely easier than striking straight up the hillside to the ridge which only leads to a confusion of large boulders and false summits for which no one should be grateful. Even so on any line of ascent the going becomes rough near the summit.

DISTANCE: 3.25 kilometres (2 miles)
ASCENT: 815 metres (2670 feet)

Route 2.13 Gallt yr Ogof from Capel Curig The *Cliff of the Cave*, Gallt yr Ogof, (so named from the conspicuous cave in its face overlooking the A5 Holyhead to London road), is an impressive bulk of mountain, and is especially well seen from the lower slopes of the mountains, Creigiau Gleision and Pen Llithrig y Wrach, across the valley. The ascent from the village of Capel Curig, using the ridge Cefn y Capel, allows the size of the mountain to be fully appreciated as one approaches.

The route is not difficult, though in places it is pathless, and begins down the lane behind the post office in Capel Curig (721582). Continue along the lane at least until after the last cottage, or until the wall ends, and then start ascending steeper ground through minor rocky outcrops.

Once the ridge has been gained – an excellent vantage point for viewing the enormity of Moel Siabod across the intervening Nantgwryd – it is a simple matter to follow its direction until steeper ground leads across the top of Nant y Gors to the summit.

From the summit, Nant y Gors may be used as a way of descent in preference to returning along the ridge, but the descent is steep in places with rocky outcrops, and requires care at all times.

DISTANCE: 4 kilometres (2.5 miles)
ASCENT: 570 metres (1870 feet)

Route 2.14 Nameless Peak and Gallt yr Ogof Combining these two peaks, which are much less frequented than all the other summits of the Glyders, makes a satisfying short excursion for walkers based at Capel Curig. From this direction it is a matter simply of following Route 2.13 to the summit of Gallt yr Ogof and then heading southwest along the connecting ridge to the slightly higher summit. There is nothing of difficulty encountered en route, and a direct return across broken ground to join Cefn y Capel takes out a little of the distance. It is worth noting that all this ground south of the watershed belongs to the Dyffryn Mymbyr farm, made famous in Thomas Firbank's book, *I Bought a Mountain*, so strictly speaking one is not entirely as free to wander as one might like. Still resident at the farm is Firbank's wife, Esme, now remarried, who as Mrs Esme Kirby is the Chairperson of the Snowdonia National Park Society. Everyone who walks in these mountains or is concerned for the future of an unspoilt Snowdonia should support this energetic Society. If you would like more information send for their lively, provocative Annual Report, List of Excursions, etc., to The Snowdonia National Park Society, Capel Curig, Betws y Coed, North Wales.

Walkers based at Ogwen can enjoy a finer walk to Nameless Peak and Gallt yr Ogof by starting from the Youth Hostel and following the Miners' Track (Route 2.1) to the plateau containing Llyn Caseg Fraith, *Lake of the Piebald Mare*. From the rim of Cwm Tryfan descend towards the lake, keeping it on the left, and pick up a broad track ascending Nameless Peak. The intervening section of ground between the two mountains presents little difficulty.

From the summit of Gallt yr Ogof it is debatable which way of returning to Ogwen is the better. To go north-west into Nant yr Ogof is rough and rarely dry, while heading north-east into Nant y Gors entails a rather steeper descent and a longer walk round. It is a question of personal preference, and in either case, the track to Gwern Gof Isaf Farm is not far away and leads on to the A5 road.

DISTANCE: (1) From Capel Curig to Nameless Peak: 5 kilometres (3.1 miles)
(2) From Ogwen to Gallt yr Ogof: 4.5 kilometres (2.8 miles)

ASCENT: (1) 615 metres (2020 feet)
(2) 600 metres (1970 feet)

Section 3 – Carneddau

	MAP REFERENCE	HEIGHT (m)	1:50 000 OS MAP
Carnedd Llywelyn	684644	1064	115
Carnedd Dafydd	663631	1044	115
Pen yr Ole Wen	656619	978	115
Foel Grach	689659	976	115
Yr Elen	674651	962	115
Foel Fras	696682	942	115
Garnedd Uchaf	687669	926	115
Llwytmor	689692	849	115
Pen yr Helgi Du	698630	833	115
Bera Bach	672678	807	115
Pen Llithrig y Wrach	716623	799	115
Bera Mawr	675683	794	115
Drum	708696	770	115

Drosgl	664680	758	115
Creigiau Gleision	729615	678	115
Unnamed summit			
(Creigiau Gleision)	734622	634	115
Pen y Castell	722689	623	115
Tal y Fan	729727	610	115
Foel Lwyd	720723	603	115

ROUTES

3.1   Carnedd Llywelyn from Helyg
3.2   Carnedd Llywelyn via Yr Elen from Gerlan
3.3   Carnedd Llywelyn from Aber
3.4   Pen yr Ole Wen from Ogwen
3.5   Pen yr Ole Wen from Tal y Llyn Ogwen
3.6   The central ridge of the Carneddau from Pen yr Ole Wen
     to Drum
3.7   The Cwm Eigiau Horseshoe
3.8   Pen y Castell and Drum
3.9   Tal y Fan
3.10 Creigiau Gleision
3.11 Pen Llithrig y Wrach
3.12 Pen yr Helgi Du
3.13 Bera Mawr and Bera Bach

Although the whole Carneddau range is liberally scattered with outcrops of rock – in many places, but especially on Craig yr Ysfa and Ysgolion Duon, presenting rock faces sufficiently severe to attract the rock-climbing fraternity – the area is essentially one of rounded, grassy hills. The central ridge, stretching from Pen yr Ole Wen in the south, for some 16 kilometres (10 miles) to the isolated summit of Tal y Fan in the north, is mostly a series of whaleback ridges and, in misty conditions, potentially dangerous. On no other range of mountains have I ever been lost, or experienced both total white-out conditions and complete disorientation; the Carneddau have obliged me with all three undesirable facets of hill walking! Most of the difficulties of this nature lie north of the highest summit, Carnedd Llywelyn, but the stretch south to Pen

yr Ole Wen has its problems too. Here the broad, feature-
less ridges of the north give way to narrower, more
convoluted ridges, with long, steep drops on both sides.
There is also something curious about the way it is all too
easy to miscalculate time and distance, and to be led into
attempting more than is reasonable.

If this gentle warning is heeded, walkers will then find
that these high mountains (two of them over 1000 metres,
and the rest not far below) afford a wide choice of routes,
not all of which are detailed here, and offer hours of
pleasurable tramping. The wild, northern valleys offer
peaceful desolation that is only matched among the
Cwmdeuddwr hills west of Rhayader and along the Elan
and Ystwyth valleys.

There is, too, much of local interest. The hills have been
inhabited since the Bronze Age, the Romans found a way
through them at Bwlch y Ddeufaen, the Druids used Tal y
Fan for some of their rites, and the highest of them,
Carnedd Llywelyn, is reputed by a religious sect based in
Los Angeles to be one of nineteen holy mountains in the
world, being charged with cosmic powers which endow
visitors with the cosmic energy to give enlightenment and
unselfish service to mankind – which is precisely why I am
writing this book; QED!

Route 3.1 Carnedd Llywelyn from Helyg Helyg is the
Climbers' Club hut adjoining the A5 at 691602, and close
by on the opposite side of the road a relatively new road,
leading to Ffynnon Llugwy reservoir, now affords easy
access to this part of the mountain range, and gives the
shortest ascent of the highest summit of the range, Carnedd Llywelyn.

Rough ground rising to Craig Wen, south of Creigiau Gleision. ▲

Carnedd Llywelyn, the highest of the Carneddau, has a special appeal ▶
under early spring snow.

Follow the access road until, approaching the as-yet-hidden reservoir, it levels and turns left to pass around a small hillock. Here take a narrow path ascending diagonally upwards, ahead and right, to Bwlch Eryl Farchog. This col, known to climbers simply as The Saddle (693634), is conspicuous throughout the approach, and lies between Pen yr Helgi Du (the long whaleback mountain on the right) and the rocky crown marking the top of Craig yr Ysfa. The upper section just below the col, once notoriously loose, is now retained in wire netting to stabilise the screes and prevent further erosion.

From the col a narrow and, in high winds or icy conditions, tricky ridge leads to the top of Craig yr Ysfa, and affords an impressive view of this popular playground. But this short ridge section does require care, more so in descent than on the way up, and nearby gullies can be a little intimidating.

Above Craig yr Ysfa the ground rises steadily, and without further ado, to the summit of Carnedd Llywelyn.
DISTANCE: 5 kilometres (3.1 miles)
ASCENT: 775 metres (2540 feet)

Because Carnedd Llywelyn is higher than adjoining mountains it is difficult even on a clear day to be absolutely sure of the correct line to take in descent. This is especially so for walkers heading to Foel Grach or Yr Elen, but not much less so for the direction to Carnedd Dafydd. A compass bearing resolves the difficulties, and in misty conditions is vital, even if you are only retracing your steps to Craig yr Ysfa.

Route 3.2 Carnedd Llywelyn via Yr Elen from Gerlan
The ascent of Yr Elen – the sore thumb of the Welsh three-thousanders, sticking out awkwardly as it does from the main Carneddau ridge – and with it the continuation to Carnedd Llywelyn itself, is one of the wild gems of North Wales. From Gerlan, near Bethesda, the route takes you into the long valley of the Llafar, leading to the towering

The Saddle between Carnedd Llywelyn and Pen yr Helgi Du.

cliffs of Ysgolion Duon, *Black Ladders*, with the unending bulk of Carnedd Dafydd swelling on the right, and the graceful lines of Yr Elen on the left. It is a desolate, unvisited place most of the year, with only the occasional, adventuresome walker trekking in among the wild ponies and the bubbling streams, though there are signs that its popularity is on the increase.

Leave Bethesda along a minor road, opposite the Bethesda Chapel and close to the post office, and continue south-east to Gerlan and the junction of roads at 633663, where at the most only two cars may be parked. Stay with the road running south-east, which twists across the Afon Caseg, and climbs to the Bangor Water Works (not identified on the 1:50000 map) just across the Afon Llafar. Here take a stile, on the right, and follow the edge of the field to a ruined cottage and another stile giving access to more open countryside. The way ahead, initially through

Pen yr Helgi Du and Pen Llithrig y Wrach are enjoyable walking in good winter conditions.

Retrospect to Pen yr Helgi Du and Pen Llithrig y Wrach from near the summit of Carnedd Llywelyn.

derelict enclosures, follows the course of the Afon Llafar, and climbs steadily as Yr Elen increases in size on the left.

The path into Cwm Llafar becomes more positive the further you go, but when it begins to descend, as the adjoining mountains start to close in, it is time to cross the river and a subsequent stretch of trackless, marshy ground, to gain the lower end of the ridge rising over two intermediate bumps to a final steep slog up to the neat summit of Yr Elen. The summit is a remarkable place, one of the most relaxing (given the right weather conditions) in the whole of Wales. Beneath the severe eastern prospect of Yr Elen nestles tiny Ffynnon Caseg, while beyond the intervening cwm swell the domes of Foel Grach, Foel Fras and the rest of the northern Carneddau.

DISTANCE: 4.25 kilometres (2.7 miles)
ASCENT: 750 metres (2460 feet)

The continuation to Carnedd Llywelyn is by a delectable narrow ridge, much too short for prolonged pleasure, but with all the attendant dangers of ridge walks elsewhere. The direction starts off a little east of south from Yr Elen, later swinging south-east to climb to the flat plateau of Carnedd Llywelyn.

DISTANCE: 1.5 kilometres (0.9 miles)
ASCENT: 155 metres (510 feet)

Route 3.3 Carnedd Llywelyn from Aber It was at Aber on the North Wales coast that Llywelyn the Great (1194–1240), one of the last native Princes of Wales, held court. And it was on the highest summit of the range of hills surrounding and protecting him that he constructed an observation post. It is tempting then, and not all that fanciful, to believe that Carnedd Llywelyn was named after him.

To ascend to Carnedd Llywelyn from Aber is no modest undertaking in terms of distance and ascent; it is something which groups of hardy fell-runners do every year in June as part of the Welsh 1000-metres Race, which eventually takes them on to the summit of Snowdon. But for less stoical individuals the ascent to Carnedd Llywelyn is adequate excursion for a day.

Start from the car park at Bont Newydd (663720), pass through the iron gate nearby, and on to a track leading to a bridge across the fast-flowing Afon Rhaeadr-fawr. This same point (just after crossing the river) may be reached by first crossing the road bridge (Bont Newydd itself) at the car park, and then turning immediately right into Forestry Commission land at a nice example of a water wheel. These two tracks soon combine, and from here, much broader now, swing right and head towards the justly famous Aber Falls.

The way up to the foot of the falls passes through a delightful, wide valley, popular with tourists, but both the valley and the tourists can be shunned in favour of relative tranquillity by taking a rising track, left, just as soon as the cottage, Nant Rhaeadr (described only as 'Nant' on the 1:50 000 map) comes fully into view, about one kilometre (0.6 miles) from Bont Newydd. This track leads first along the edge of a forest, and later enters it at a stile, leading peacefully through pine plantations to emerge close to a wide span of screes falling from crags above to the valley below the falls. The path continues horizontally across the screes, with care being needed in one or two places until the scree is behind you. From the valley bottom, for those who have travelled this way, a laborious ascent of the treadmill is required, making this a better option for descent.

Once across the screes, continue on a clear path, climbing steadily, twisting around gullies and rock outcrops, and passing a particularly treacherous few metres where water, seeping for years across slanting rocks, has created a tilted, slimy barrier to the gorge above the falls. Great care is needed here.

The path soon climbs above the falls and into a long, hanging valley down which the Afon Goch tumbles happily. Walkers taking to Bera Mawr or Llwytmor can opt out of the valley here, but those continuing to Carnedd Llywelyn should pursue the valley for its entire length, only leaving it, by ascending right, as it starts to widen out. This gives a route with no views, but, to commend it, it is sheltered from the prevailing winds. Stay with the streams in the upper part of the valley for as long as possible, finally leaving them to head for the rocky outcrop, Yr Aryg, or to the minor summit, Garnedd Uchaf, where the main central ridge of the Carneddau is joined.

A line almost due south from Garnedd Uchaf will lead first to the stone shelter on Foel Grach, and then by ascending grassy slopes to Carnedd Llywelyn. The comments made in the introduction about route finding are especially important if mist is encountered after leaving the Aber gorge.

DISTANCE: 8.5 kilometres (5.3 miles)
ASCENT: 1000 metres (3280 feet)

Route 3.4 Pen yr Ole Wen from Ogwen Pen yr Ole Wen is the southern end of the long central ridge of the Carneddau. From the Ogwen Falls, where they plunge over the great step at the head of Nant Ffrancon, a broad, bare, exposed shoulder of rock and scree sufficient to test the stamina of anyone, shoots upwards for 675 metres. Views en route, and taking time to admire them is likely to be a popular pursuit, are of the high cwms of the northern Glyders, Idwal, and the imposing tower of Tryfan behind which rise the Glyders themselves, massive and grey.

Near the telephone box at the side of the A5, pass through a gap in the wall on the opposite side of the road and pick a way through the spread of broken outcrops to gain a more conspicuous track, steep and loose, working a way up the mountainside. It is hard work, rewarded only by directness, but beware! . . . the apparent summit, in sight for most of the way, really is only apparent. From it the hillside leans back, demanding quite a deal more plodding before the top of the mountain is reached. And even then, resting by a cairn and small shelter, it is

The long whaleback ridge of Pen yr Helgi Du beneath which shelters the Ffynnon Llugwy reservoir.

The final stretch to the summit of Carnedd Llywelyn on the ascent from Helyg.

The northern Carneddau from near the summit of Carnedd Llywelyn.

The sun highlights the long ridge, above Ysgolion Duon, between Carnedd Llywelyn and Carnedd Dafydd. The summit of Glyder Fach is silhouetted in the left background, and Heather Terrace can just be made out crossing the east face of Tryfan.

The Afon Goch, just above the Aber Falls, with Bera Mawr in the distance.

The craggy summit of Bera Mawr and Bera Bach.

Wild moorland around the Afon Llafar, rising to distant Yr Elen.

easy to see that higher ground lies further north-east.
DISTANCE: 1.75 kilometres (1.1 miles)
ASCENT: 675 metres (2215 feet)

Route 3.5 Pen yr Ole Wen from Tal y Llyn Ogwen
Walkers wishing to avoid the brutality of the direct ascent
of Pen yr Ole Wen from Ogwen, will find the way up from
the other end of the lake, at Tal y Llyn Ogwen (668605),
significantly easier and more rewarding.

Follow the track to the farm where the route is way-
marked through the *ffridd*, or intake as it is known
in England, and on to the open hillside, keeping close to
the line of the Afon Lloer. The path is often vague,
and initially is quite a grind, but the tedium dissolves as
soon as it becomes possible to move left to gain the spur
thrown down to the east by Pen yr Ole Wen. Some easy
navigation through rocks leads on to the upper part of
the spur, with a surprise view of Ffynnon Lloer cradled

in the cwm below, and then on to the summit.
DISTANCE: 2.5 kilometres (1.6 miles)
ASCENT: 675 metres (2215 feet)

Route 3.6 The central ridge of the Carneddau from Pen yr Ole Wen to Drum It matters not which way round you tackle this connoisseur's pride, either way presents transport problems. This south-to-north traverse is given simply because it gives the impression of getting easier as you go on.

Either of the ascents to Pen yr Ole Wen will suffice to start, but Route 3.5 is marginally easier. From this first summit continue around the upper rim of Cwm Ffynnon Lloer to the minor intermediate top, Garnedd Fach, and then on to Carnedd Dafydd – a summit named after the penultimate native Prince of Wales.

From Carnedd Dafydd the section to the highest summit, Carnedd Llywelyn, is especially rewarding, taking you across the top of Ysgolion Duon, *Black Ladders*, with extensive views down Cwm Llafar to distant Anglesey and Puffin Island. After the Black Ladders the ridge narrows dramatically across Bwlch Cyfryr-Drum (not named on the 1:50000 map), before it climbs to the rocky plateau of Carnedd Llywelyn. Escape from Carnedd Dafydd in bad weather is best effected by continuing east along the ridge for about half a kilometre (a quarter of a mile) and then descending south to Tal y Llyn Ogwen on relatively easy slopes; but keep well away from the boulder and scree slopes directly above Ffynnon Lloer.

There is the option at Carnedd Llywelyn of extending the crossing to include the remote summit of Yr Elen, a welcome diversion on a crowded summer's day. On from Carnedd Llywelyn the ridge broadens considerably, and in mist calls for a spot of compass work to hit the Refuge Hut on Foel Grach. A line of standing stones, occasionally knocked down, intercepts the path along the ridge, lead-

Yr Elen from the north. ▶

ing you to the hut. But on a clear day you can divert from the main line to gaze down into the dark waters of Llyn Dulyn and Melynllyn, lying in an area known to have been inhabited during the Bronze Age.

The summit of Foel Fras, the next mountain along the ridge (discounting the insignificant Garnedd Uchaf), is unimpressive, and lies close to a stone wall. Again the way to it will have been made easier in misty conditions by the odd compass bearing.

Beyond Foel Fras lies Drum from where a descent over Carnedd y Ddelw and Drosgl to the roadhead at Bwlch y Ddeufaen is easily accomplished.

DISTANCE: 16 kilometres (10 miles)
ASCENT: 1080 metres (3540 feet)

Route 3.7 The Cwm Eigiau Horseshoe This circular walk starting in one of the more remote and less visited areas of the Carneddau is one of the classic walks of Wales, possessing soaring ridges, narrow arêtes, high mountains and breathtaking scenery. It is certainly more popular than it was even ten years ago, and so it deserves to be. This is that superb summer's day walk over which you can dawdle, or on which to test winter stamina in what then becomes a whole new ball-game.

From Tal y Bont in the Vale of Conwy take the minor road between the Afon Dulyn and the Afon Porth-llwyd to 732663, where the road ends, and start from here. The hillsides are dotted with ruins, long since vacated in the unequal struggle between man and the elements, their owners and occupiers leaving the area more devoid of life than it has been probably since the Bronze Age.

Take the stony track on the south to Hafod-y-rhiw, there leaving it to climb the long, broad, ascending ridge to Pen Llithrig y Wrach, with Snowdonia's deepest lake, Llyn Cowlyd, and the bumpy ridge of Creigiau Gleision to the south-east. From Pen Llithrig y Wrach descend north of west to Bwlch y Trimarchog, *Pass of the Three Horsemen*, where boundaries, quite possibly settled long ago by three local landowners on horseback, meet. Then take a short, steep climb to the spacious top of Pen yr Helgi Du.

A few steps northward from the small cairn on Pen yr Helgi Du reveal a striking change. Below, seen for the first time, are the dark waters of Ffynnon Llugwy, while nearer to hand the ridge at your feet plummets abruptly to the knife edge arête of The Saddle (693634). The descent is not so long as might be imagined, but the difficulties are there, and hands are needed in places. Beyond, the ridge climbs to the top of Craig yr Ysfa to expose the dramatic view of steep cliffs on which rock climbers find their sport.

The continuation to Carnedd Llywelyn more or less follows the rim of upper Cwm Eigiau where, one superb winter's day, with crisp snow under foot and a wealth of photographs all around, I celebrated running out of film in both my cameras by flinging them to the ground in disgust, thankful moments later that the crispness still had a few holes in it to cushion my frustration!

Mention has been made elsewhere of the need to check bearings before trying to leave the summit of Carnedd Llywelyn; being higher than surrounding mountains the onward view is momentarily out of sight. The way to Foel Grach however, once established, poses no problems, and a diversion, right, to investigate a conspicuous rock tower will reveal piles of stones and the remains of a circular burial mound. Some stories claim this as the burial place of Tristan, of Arthurian legend. More likely, as with other similar sites in the Carneddau, it dates from the Bronze Age.

From Foel Grach, and its often grotty Refuge Hut, retreat south-east to gain the long ridge curling round Melynllyn. The walled enclosures of the Bronze-Age settlement near the Dulyn reservoir are normally easily seen from this ridge, and cause you to reflect for a while on life as it must have been then, when the facility of returning home to a warm bath and food after a cold day in the hills was as distant as time itself.

Trend right, across the ridge, and descend steeply to the

ruins of Tal y Llyn, from where the roadhead is easily regained.

DISTANCE: 14.5 kilometres (9 miles)
ASCENT: 1015 metres (3330 feet)

Route 3.8 Pen y Castell and Drum As much as anywhere else in the Carneddau, Pen y Castell has an eery feeling of remoteness, yet, with the broad expanse of the Conwy valley clearly in view, it is easily achieved, even at a leisurely pace, and is much closer to civilisation than other spots in these wide-ranging hills.

Leave the Vale of Conwy at Tal y Bont, and climb past Ye Olde Bull Inn at Llanbedr y Cennin to a fork at 749699. Take the left fork to a spot just above Bwlch y Gaer farm where a few cars can be parked, and start from here. Nearby, by way of a diversion before you start, is Pen y Gaer (750694), a fine example of an elaborate Iron-Age defence system around a hill fort with stone circles. This can be reached by continuing along the road for a short distance to a stile, and then pursuing a path up the hill.

For Pen y Castell, take the rough track ascending gently in a south-westerly direction until, at the third gate, it meets a wall descending from near the summit of Pen y Castell. Pass through the gate (to avoid having to climb the wall later), cross a fence at a makeshift stile, and follow the wall upwards on a vague path. After the initial steepness the wall changes direction abruptly, and does not extend all the way to the summit. But the neat, rocky top of Pen y Castell is directly ahead, and finding it should present no difficulties.

DISTANCE: 2.25 kilometres (1.4 miles)
ASCENT: 265 metres (870 feet)

The continuation to Drum is north-west, and trackless, involving only a steady rise to the summit. Carnedd Penydorth Goch is the alternative name for Drum, the highest point of which is the site of a Bronze-Age platform, roughly circular and about 18 metres (60 feet) in diameter.

Nearby, the minor top, Carnedd y Ddelw, *Cairn of the Image*, is the site of a Bronze-Age cist where a small golden figurine, five inches in length, was discovered in the eighteenth century.

DISTANCE: 1.75 kilometres (1.1 miles)
ASCENT: 180 metres (590 feet)

From Drum the way is open: south, along the central Carneddau ridge to Foel Fras and beyond, north, over Carnedd y Ddelw and Drosgl to Bwlch y Ddeufaen, *Pass of the Two Stones*, invaded now by electricity pylons in much the same way, though with noticeably less concern for visual amenity, that it was centuries ago by the Romans who found this weakness in the hills a way of circumventing the difficulties of Penmaenmawr.

Route 3.9 Tal y Fan Seeming to dominate the holiday town of Conwy, Tal y Fan and the adjacent Foel Lwyd assume greater proportions than they actually possess. They form the last link in a chain of hills stretching roughly south-westward for many kilometres to Pen yr Ole Wen high above the Ogwen valley. Between Tal y Fan and the rest of the Carneddau lies the gap of Bwlch y Ddeufaen, *Pass of the Two Stones*, so named from the presence there of two prehistoric monoliths of uncertain date standing to the east of the highest point of the Roman road which passes through the gap. There is little evidence of the original Roman road today but it is known that they used this high pass as a means of access to the westerly parts of the North Wales coast from their fort at Caerhun (Canovium) in the Vale of Conwy.

Tal y Fan may easily be ascended from the top of the pass, which can almost be reached by car from Llanbedr y Cennin. But there are many ways to this popular summit, particularly from Conwy and Llanfairfechan.

From Llanfairfechan, start along the minor road from the traffic lights, and, on leaving habitation behind, follow the course of the Afon Ddu either to the top of the pass, or leave the river in its lower reaches and take a direct line, mostly over dry grass to the col between Tal y Fan and Foel Lwyd. Walkers ascending to the top of the pass should then follow the wall upwards, keeping on its north side to avoid having to negotiate other walls later. The second summit, Foel Lwyd (only shown as spot height 598 on the 1:50 000 map), is crossed first.

DISTANCE: 6 kilometres (3.75 miles)
ASCENT: 585 metres (1920 feet)

From Bont Newydd at Aber, cross the bridge and follow the road until it ends. Turn left and climb to a stile, after which gain a wide track curling around the minor top, Foel Ganol, and heading for Bwlch y Ddeufaen. Then ascend on the north side of the wall as described above.

DISTANCE: 7.5 kilometres (4.7 miles)
ASCENT: 545 metres (1790 feet)

Variations to this route can be made to include Drum, either by the beautiful valley of the Afon Anafon, or by taking the track heading south from spot height 393 just north of Foel Ganol.

Route 3.10 Creigiau Gleision Separated from the rest of the Carneddau by the deepest lake in Snowdonia, Llyn Cowlyd, Creigiau Gleision is in some ways an isolated summit. But its proximity to Capel Curig, and the exceedingly rugged terrain around it, continue to make this double-topped peak a popular excursion with walkers who enjoy the ups and downs of mountain life. An elongated, undulating ridge with a proliferation of minor bumps and hollows eventually gets you where you want to be, and gives an insight into rather less rounded, grassy country than is encountered elsewhere in this immense range of hills.

Start over the stile opposite the post office in Capel Curig, and take the track past The Pinnacles, the conspicuous rock-climbing training ground used by nearby Plas y

Brenin Mountain Centre. Just after The Pinnacles turn left, searching a little for stiles that are not obvious, and continue to the minor top, Crimpiau (733596), on the way to which there is a small lake, Llyn y Coryn (731591 – not shown on the 1:50000 map). To reach Creigiau Gleision it is not necessary to take in the actual summit of Crimpiau since a descending path crosses its north-west flank and leads to the col overlooking Llyn Crafnant to the north-east.

Yet another minor top, Craig Wen, looms between Crimpiau and Creigiau Gleision, but beyond, after a short descent to another col, Bwlch Mignog (not named on the 1:50000 map), an easy ascent over grass and rock leads to the small cairn on the main summit.

DISTANCE: 4 kilometres (2.5 miles)
ASCENT: 480 metres (1575 feet)

The unnamed summit on Creigiau Gleision lies a short distance north-east over an intervening bump, and leads on to an excellent long walk to the dam of Llyn Cowlyd, returning either along the lake shore, or, for the super fit, over Pen Llithrig y Wrach. Rather than tackle a direct descent to the dam, it is better to follow an old fence-line from the end of the summit ridge, leading in the direction of Llyn Crafnant, and then, before Pen y Graig-gron is reached, turning left to descend a wide gulley to reach the dam over deep, trackless heather.

Route 3.11 Pen Llithrig y Wrach From where the name, *Slippery Hill of the Witch*, derives is uncertain, but there is something hunched and witch-like in its profile when seen across Llyn Eigiau from near Pen y Castell. It is strong in profile, too, from the vicinity of Capel Curig, where it appears as a squat pyramid rising above bleak moorland. It is from this direction that the most direct ascent can be made.

Leave the A5 at Bron Heulog (720588), and take the signposted path, wet and boggy in places, to the inflow to the Llyn Cowlyd reservoir. Cross the man-made leat connecting Cowlyd with Ffynnon Llugwy at 716609, and ascend the hillside ahead to the summit. The view down the length of Llyn Cowlyd is very impressive, hemmed in to the south-east by the rugged shape of Creigiau Gleision, but extending for many kilometres north-eastwards.

DISTANCE: 3.75 kilometres (2.3 miles)
ASCENT: 570 metres (1870 feet)

A better way to visit Pen Llithrig y Wrach than this simple, direct ascent is to make use of the col to the west, Bwlch y Trimarchog, and join it with Pen yr Helgi Du – a suggestion put to good use in the tour of the Cwm Eigiau Horseshoe (see Route 3.7).

Route 3.12 Pen yr Helgi Du The *Hill of the Black Hound*, Pen yr Helgi Du, forms an elongated whaleback ridge rising north from the Ogwen valley, from where it may easily be ascended. There are two popular routes to the summit, both starting along the reservoir road described in Route 3.1, which leaves the A5 at 687603.

3.12a Follow Route 3.1 to The Saddle, between Craig yr Ysfa and Pen yr Helgi Du. This connecting ridge is narrow, and especially impressive when under snow, but lovers of this type of situation will find it woefully lacking in length. From the col, go right, to a pleasant, short scramble to the summit.

DISTANCE: 3.5 kilometres (2.2 miles)
ASCENT: 545 metres (1790 feet)

3.12b Leave the reservoir road at the leat connecting the Ffynnon Llugwy reservoir with Llyn Cowlyd, and follow a path along the leat until two bridges are encountered. Cross the leat by the second bridge and ascend diagonally

Aber Falls, one of North Wales' most famous waterfalls.

right to gain the southern end of the long ridge just north of Tal y Braich farm. Once on the ridge a path will be found, leading directly to the summit.

DISTANCE: 3.5 kilometres (2.2 miles)

ASCENT: 545 metres (1790 feet)

Pen yr Helgi Du is often linked with its neighbouring summit, Pen Llithrig y Wrach, *Slippery Hill of the Witch*, and the descent to the connecting col, Bwlch y Trimarchog, starts south-west of the summit of Pen yr Helgi Du and is marked by a large cairn.

Route 3.13 Bera Mawr and Bera Bach The words 'Mawr' and 'Bach' here mean 'large' and 'small' respectively, which makes the fact that Bera Bach is the higher summit of the two a little confusing. It could simply be that Bera Mawr is given preference because it is the only one seen from the valley below the Aber Falls, from where it does indeed appear very large, and sometimes not a little daunting. Or it may be that the discrepancy has only been revealed by modern surveying techniques. Whatever the reason it has no bearing on the appeal of these two comparatively isolated summits of the Carneddau as an excellent short excursion. 'Short' here is a relative term, for although the distance involved may not be great, the ascent has the knack of taking a lot of steam out of your legs.

Start from the car park at Bont Newydd and pursue Route 3.3 until the hanging valley above the Aber Falls is reached. Then, at the first opportunity to cross the Afon Goch safely, do so and climb to Bera Mawr's north-west ridge, and then on to the summit over untracked moorland. If a crossing of the Afon Goch near to the falls does not appeal, continue into the valley for about 2 kilometres (1.25 miles), without significant ascent, until the river narrows and it becomes possible to pull up to Bera Mawr from the east. There is not much to choose between either alternative, but crossing the Afon Goch can be problem-

atical as I discovered in 1970 when I measured my length across the river's greater width, much to the amusement of my companion, who laughed so much he fell in himself!
DISTANCE: 4 kilometres (2.5 miles)
ASCENT: 720 metres (2360 feet)

The summit of nearby Bera Bach, like its companion Bera Mawr, is a confused tumble of rocks from which project castellated arrangements to amuse would-be rock climbers. Neither summit, both being narrow points of rock, is marked. The continuation between the two presents no problems, though it is frequently wet, some of which can be avoided by contouring around the higher ground rather than trying to take a direct route.
DISTANCE: 0.75 kilometres (0.5 miles)
ASCENT: 45 metres (145 feet)

Mynydd Mawr, Craig y Bera, and the upper Nantlle valley, seen from the summit of Y Garn at the end of the Nantlle ridge.

Section 4 – Hebog and Nantlle

	MAP REFERENCE	HEIGHT (m)	1:50 000 OS MAP
Hebog			
Moel Hebog	565469	783	115
Moel yr Ogof	556478	655	115
Moel Lefn	553485	638	115
Nantlle			
Craig Cwm Silyn	525503	734	115
Trum y Ddysgl	545516	709	115
Garnedd Goch	511495	701	115
Mynydd Mawr	539547	698	115
Mynydd Drws y Coed	549518	695	115
Mynydd Tal y Mignedd	535514	653	115
Y Garn	551526	633	115
Mynydd Craig Goch	497485	609	115/123

ROUTES

4.1 Moel Hebog, Moel yr Ogof and Moel Lefn from Beddgelert

4.2 The Nantlle ridge

4.3 Mynydd Mawr

The hills of the Hebog and Nantlle ranges, which are more correctly (but not generally) known as the Eifionydd Hills, in no way let down the high standard of hill-walking country in North Wales. The Nantlle ridge is every bit as rewarding as anything in Snowdonia, indeed as anything in the whole of Wales, while Mynydd Mawr lying to the north has an untroubled air for walkers who want peace and quiet.

Until the late 1970s the Nantlle ridge was forbidden country, and it was only by the diligent efforts of the Snowdonia National Park Authority that access arrangements have been agreed with the landowners, a concession that must be respected.

The views from the whole group of hills are superb: south-west rise the conical summits of The Rivals along the Lleyn Peninsula, while to the east the bulk of the

Snowdon massif fills the horizon. To the north the view extends across the whole length of Anglesey, and to the south-east reaches over the intermediate heights of Cnicht and the Moelwyns to give occasional glimpses of the Cader Idris range and beyond.

Route 4.1 Moel Hebog, Moel yr Ogof and Moel Lefn
The traverse of these three hills near the village of Beddgelert is an entertaining trip with excellent views and without any undue difficulty, though some steep descents can be tiring and tricky in adverse weather conditions.

Start at a small car park just off the A498 in Beddgelert, and pass along the northern gable of the Royal Goat Hotel into a small, modern housing estate. Look for a signpost (Llwybr Cyhoeddus) on the right and a pedestrian way-marker between the houses at the top of the estate, which point the way to a bridge over the disused Welsh Highland Railway. Cross a stile and turn right to follow a walled path to another stile, where you join a rough road. Go left along the road, through a small section of forest to a stile at 581478 adjacent to farm buildings. Here cross a boggy field (way-marked) to the broad ridge seen descending from Moel Hebog's summit. Follow a path up the ridge. The angle never eases, but there are many places to stop and admire the fine retrospective view over Yr Aran and Snowdon, with Glyder Fach just getting a look in through the gaps.

Near the top of the ridge the path is broken and rocky, and leads to the top of Diffwys (not named on the 1:50 000 map), the prominent cliff facing north-east to Snowdon. From here follow an obvious path up a short, rocky section to the top.

The summit is marked by a trig point near a stone wall.
DISTANCE: 3 kilometres (1.9 miles)
ASCENT: 750 metres (2460 feet)

Moel yr Ogof, *Hill of the Cave*, (unnamed on the 1:50 000 map), commemorates a hiding place of Owain Glyndŵr, which is marked. To continue to Moel yr Ogof descend steeply on grass north-westwards following the line of a wall to the bwlch between Cwm Pennant to the south-west and Cwm Meillionen to the north-east. From the bwlch there is an easy climb, passing a small lake in a hidden hollow, to the summit. On this section of the walk, particularly on the slopes beyond the lake, it is quite easy to find fossils, demonstrating that this area was at one time entirely beneath the sea.

DISTANCE: 1.5 kilometres (0.9 miles)
ASCENT: 120 metres (390 feet)

On further still lies Moel Lefn, the last outpost before the splendid walking of the Nantlle ridge. The ascent of Moel Lefn from Moel yr Ogof will present no problems, and the views to the north become better all the time.

DISTANCE: 0.75 kilometres (0.5 miles)
ASCENT: 75 metres (250 feet)

From the summit descend steeply to the corner of the forest at 554496, just south of the heathery knoll, Y Gyrn (553501, but unnamed on the 1:50000 map). Enter the forest, and pick up a footpath through the trees. After a while this leaves the forest (at a stile) for a short distance before re-entering it. For the most part ignore the main forest trails, though they will get you out of the forest if you lose your way, eventually! Keep instead to the foot-paths, many of which are way-marked and very enjoyable, especially in hot weather. A general downward trend leads to a camp-site at 576491, from where a track southwards will lead back to Beddgelert, rejoining the track used on the ascent of Moel Hebog.

Route 4.2 The Nantlle ridge In the whole of North Wales the Nantlle ridge is only surpassed in unadulterated walking pleasure by the Snowdon Horseshoe, yet it is a neglected excursion. Perhaps this is because it is one long ridge, rather than a circuit, and walkers therefore have the problem either of being met at the end, or of retracing their steps – not that there is anything wrong with the latter! The walk is described here from east to west, with the addition of lines of ascent from the west for those who find it convenient to start from that end.

The first summit is Y Garn, a name that crops up quite often in Wales, because it's the word English anglicises as 'cairn', but it is little more than an extension of the next mountain along the ridge, Mynydd Drws y Coed. Start from the National Park car park in Rhyd Ddu (572526), and take the B4418 to a gate (566526) at the sharp bend in the road barely half a kilometre (a quarter of a mile) south-west of the village. The way on to Y Garn, and the beginning of the ridge, is marked by white arrows painted on the rocks. After the second stile the path divides, the route left going across Bwlch y Ddwy Elor into Cwm Pennant, while our route ascends steeply up grassy slopes to the summit. An indication of the steepness can be assumed from the fact that this relatively short ascent can consume well over an hour's effort. The hard work however is rewarded by a dramatic view of the cliffs of Craig y Bera on the southern slopes of Mynydd Mawr, and of the tranquil scene of the Nantlle valley lying a long way below.
DISTANCE: 2.5 kilometres (1.6 miles)
ASCENT: 445 metres (1460 feet)

The continuation to Mynydd Drws y Coed, almost due south, soon turns from grass to rock, becoming steep and narrow in places, but is nowhere difficult, though the use of hands will be needed.

The summit of Mynydd Drws y Coed, a grassy elevation only a little higher than surrounding rocks, is without a cairn, but lies a few metres south of a stile crossing a boundary fence. The mountain takes its name from the farm below. Across the cwm, and in view all the time, lies the next mountain Trum y Ddysgl.
DISTANCE: 0.75 kilometres (0.5 miles)
ASCENT: 85 metres (280 feet)

Mynydd Drws y Coed and Trum y Ddysgl are the second and third summits ▶
in an east–west traverse of the Nantlle ridge.

Trum y Ddysgl, *Ridge of the Dish*, takes its name from the shape of its northern cliffs when viewed from the Nantlle valley. The summit, a small, elongated grassy ridge, is easily reached from Mynydd Drws y Coed, and leads on to a narrow grassy connection to the next summit, Mynydd Tal y Mignedd.

From the summit of Trum y Ddysgl a long, descending ridge projects southwards into the upper reaches of Cwm Pennant, meeting it at the old corpse road, Bwlch y Ddwy Elor, *Pass of the Two Biers*. Despite its deathly connotations this is a useful descent in the event of adverse weather, and will permit a low-level return to Rhyd Ddu.

DISTANCE: 0.5 kilometres (0.3 miles)
ASCENT: 40 metres (130 feet)

After the descent from Trum y Ddysgl, the ascent to Mynydd Tal y Mignedd presents no difficulty.

The absence of summit cairns on either Trum y Ddysgl or Mynydd Drws y Coed is compensated for by the one on

---

The domed, grassy summit of Trum y Ddysgl seen from near the summit of Mynydd Tal y Mignedd.

Mynydd Tal y Mignedd. Here a towering chimney-like obelisk, constructed to celebrate Queen Victoria's Jubilee, is a remarkable tribute to the quarrymen who built it.

DISTANCE: 1 kilometre (0.6 miles)
ASCENT: 40 metres (130 feet)

South-west of Mynydd Tal y Mignedd lies the col, Bwlch Dros Bern (not named on the 1:50000 map), thought to have been an old drove road from Cwm Pennant to Nantlle, though there is little evidence of that now. The descent to the bwlch is at first south, by the line of a fence, and then south-west. There are two stiles en route, one at the top of the steep, badly eroded descent to the bwlch, and the other at the bottom. Both should be used to avoid minor rock outcrops.

From the bwlch there is a rocky ascent to the wider summit of Craig Cwm Silyn at the centre of the ridge. The bwlch seems to mark a change in character; to the east the four summits are narrow and twisting, and mostly grassy

The highest summit along the Nantlle ridge, Craig Cwm Silyn.

underfoot, while to the west, the remaining three tops are wider, rockier and less serpentine.
DISTANCE: 1.5 kilometres (0.9 miles)
ASCENT: 245 metres (800 feet)

The continuation westwards to Garnedd Goch is a simple walk, a diversion from which, to the northern edge of Craig Cwm Silyn, will reveal the Great Slab, a favourite playground of rock-climbers, towering above the twin turquoise lakes in Cwm Silyn below. Onwards the route soon joins a stone wall leading to the summit of Garnedd Goch, the penultimate top in the traverse.
DISTANCE: 1.5 kilometres (0.9 miles)
ASCENT: 30 metres (100 feet)

The final summit along the ridge is Mynydd Craig Goch, a weird place of castellated and gnarled rocks overlooking the sea and the Lleyn Peninsula. To reach Mynydd Craig Goch from Garnedd Goch, descend steeply by a wall until you can conveniently cross it, and follow another wall to the col between the two mountains, Bwlch Cwmdulyn. The continuation from the bwlch is not direct, and heads first in a southerly direction before taking gently rising ground westwards.
DISTANCE: 2 kilometres (1.25 miles)
ASCENT: 75 metres (250 feet)
TOTAL DISTANCE: 9.7 kilometres (6 miles)
TOTAL ASCENT: 960 metres (3150 feet)

Walkers wishing to traverse the ridge in the opposite direction will need to make for Bwlch Cwmdulyn first, either from Nebo (478505) or from Tal y Sarn (494526).

From Nebo a road leads to the outflow of Llyn Cwmdulyn, from where a path, marked by upright stones, continues to the lower slopes of Garnedd Goch and then on to the bwlch, meeting the wall descending steeply from the summit.

From Tal y Sarn the immediate objective, which can be

The summit of Craig Cwm Silyn, with Garnedd Goch in the distance.

reached by car by leaving the Dolbebi–Llanllyfni road at 481521, is a gate across the track into Cwm Silyn at 496511. From the gate a wall can be seen ascending to Garnedd Goch. Follow this wall, across ground that is boggy in places, until it meets a higher wall with a gap in it (505503). Continue from the gap on to a path, also marked by small standing stones, until it meets with the path ascending from Nebo, then proceed to Bwlch Cwmdulyn.

Once at the bwlch the final part of the east–west traverse can be undertaken to Mynydd Craig Goch before retracing one's steps to ascend to Garnedd Goch.

Route 4.3 Mynydd Mawr This isolated mountain on the northern side of the Nantlle valley is seldom visited, but provides uncomplicated walking on predominantly grassy slopes.

Start from Planwydd Farm (568539) at the southern end of Llyn Cwellyn, and follow an obvious forest trail through the plantations until you can join the south-east ridge and climb steeply to a minor top, Foel Rudd (not named on the 1:50000 map). From Foel Rudd the track continues above the spectacular cliffs of Craig y Bera, to which a diversion may easily be made, and then on to the summit cairn of the mountain.

The views, once the forest has been left, are dominated by the undulations of the Nantlle ridge, but beneath the steep slopes of Y Garn lies the shapely lake, Llyn y Dywarchen, mentioned by Gerald of Wales in his *Journey through Wales* as possessing a floating island. Subsequent travellers, up to 600 years later, have remarked upon the island, including the famous astronomer Halley who swam out to it in 1698 to satisfy himself that it existed. The present island, despite any wishful thinking, stays put.

DISTANCE: 3.5 kilometres (2 miles)
ASCENT: 555 metres (1820 feet)

Section 5 – Siabod and the Moelwyns

	MAP REFERENCE	HEIGHT (m)	1:50000 OS MAP
Siabod			
Moel Siabod	705546	872	115
The Moelwyns			
Moelwyn Mawr	658449	770	124
Moelwyn Bach	660437	710	124
Allt Fawr	682475	698	115
Cnicht	645466	689	115
Moel Druman	671476	676	115
Ysgafell Wen	667481	672	115
Unnamed summit (Ysgafell Wen)	663485	669	115
Manod Mawr	724447	661	124
Unnamed summit (Manod Mawr)	727458	658	115

Moel yr Hydd	672454	648	115
Moel Penamnen	716483	623	115
Moel Meirch	661504	607	115

ROUTES
5.1 Moel Siabod from Capel Curig
5.2 Moelwyn Mawr and Moelwyn Bach from Croesor
5.3 Cnicht from Croesor
5.4 Ysgafell Wen and the Dog Lakes from Nanmor
5.5 Moel Meirch from Nantgwynant
5.6 Allt Fawr from the Crimea Pass
5.7 Moel yr Hydd by Cwmorthin
5.8 Moel Penamnen from the Crimea Pass
5.9 Manod Mawr

Despite having in its midst two of the most enjoyable summits in Snowdonia, Moel Siabod and Cnicht, the Moelwyn group as a whole is relatively unvisited. The unsightly, industry-scarred face the range presents from many angles is a strong deterrent for most walkers, but there still remain vast tracts of land unravaged by man and well worth exploring.

Siabod in the north, and the sham Matterhorn of Wales, Cnicht to the south, need little introduction. They are popular walks, and deservedly so, offering all that is rewarding in hill walking. But between Cnicht and Moel Siabod lies a rough, tumbling area of many lakes nestling in rocky hollows. The traverse of this area west to east from Nanmor, across Ysgafell Wen, Moel Druman and Allt Fawr, to the Crimea Pass, can usually be accomplished even in summer without encountering any other walker, and is an interesting trip.

At the extreme western end of this vast area lies the spectacular gorge of the Aberglaslyn Pass, just south of the village of Beddgelert. Nearby, rising north-east, runs the rough valley of Cwm Bychan, with which the moguls of Twentieth Century Fox were favourably impressed,

Beyond Llyn y Foel rise the hills of the Moelwyns. ▶

building here the walled Chinese city of Wangcheng for their film, *The Inn of the Sixth Happiness*. Ogwen and Nant Ffrancon also featured in the film.

The Moelwyns themselves suffer from the encroachment of industry, and the view from their tops is often dismal and scarred. But for walkers with an interest in industrial archaeology, the round of Cnicht and the Moelwyns is rewarding, passing as it does through the Rhosydd Quarry and its attendant lakes and reservoirs.

East across the valley that contains Blaenau Ffestiniog and Ffestiniog, rolls a series of minor hills stretching out to the vast, untamed bogland known as the Migneint. Principal among these hills are Manod Mawr and its unnamed partner to the north, and lonely Moel Penamnen. There are no particular long walks here, but it is possible to escape all the dereliction of the higher hills to the west.

Route 5.1 Moel Siabod from Capel Curig Moel Siabod at 872 metres is a magnificent viewpoint for the whole Snowdonia panorama, its own impression of vastness heightened by its isolation from any other mountain group. At its feet to the north lies the Dyffryn valley, Nantgwryd, while to the south stretch the wild boglands of the Moelwyns proper. East and west, along the axis of the mountain, lie the Carneddau and the Snowdon massif respectively, and across the Dyffryn valley the Glyders rise in one massive display of high mountain land. Reach the summit of Siabod on a quiet weekday, and the grandeur that is everywhere will have greater impact. On a clear day, the old guide books boasted, you could see to Cardigan Bay and the Irish Sea.

Normally Moel Siabod is ascended from Pont Cyfyng (734572), about 2 kilometres (1.25 miles) south-east of Capel Curig, at a point where the busy Afon Llugwy fights its way through a mass of huge boulders in a picturesque cascade. Cross the bridge and take the second turning on

Moel Siabod. ▶

The popular route to the summit of Moel Siabod.

Cnicht, in this shot belying the fact that it is really a long ridge.

Moel yr Hydd seen across the waters of the dammed Llyn Cwm Corsiog.

The ruins of Rhosydd Quarry buildings on the bwlch between Cwm Croesor and Cwmorthin.

the right to climb past some farm buildings and on to a disused quarry road at a stile. Just at the point on the map where the quarry is marked, the path forks. Ahead (the right fork) lies a steepish grassy ramp ascending directly on to the east ridge of the mountain. This is the customary route, but it is best left for descent, for there is a better way close by.

At the fork go left, initially on a good track passing around a lake before you climb to a steep-sided quarry lake (shown on the map). From here the path is less distinct, but there is a slight col ahead for which to aim, and once across the col the scene is magnificent. Immediately in front of you lies sombre Llyn y Foel with the Moelwyns filling the skyline beyond, while to the right rise the formidable southern flanks of Siabod with few obvious ways of ascent. But beyond the lake the mountain throws down a superb ridge, Daear Ddu (not named on the 1:50 000 map), which can be reached easily across some boggy ground, and ascended in airy fashion almost directly to the summit of the mountain.

DISTANCE: 4 kilometres (2.5 miles)
ASCENT: 690 metres (2265 feet)

Route 5.2 Moelwyn Mawr and Moelwyn Bach from Croesor The village of Croesor is an excellent place from which to start an ascent of either of the Moelwyns, with the connecting ridge between them, crossing the minor summit, Craig Ysgafn, presenting no problems.

For Moelwyn Mawr start from the car park in Croesor (631446), and return to the nearby crossroads. Take the south-east fork (ahead at the crossroads) to Pont Maesgwm (635439), shortly after which a path, crossing the Afon Maesgwm, ascends to Braich-y-parc and up the long south-west ridge to the summit trig. This, like the similar ascent of Moelwyn Bach, is pleasant walking to be taken at an easy pace.

DISTANCE: 3.75 kilometres (2.3 miles)
ASCENT: 615 metres (2020 feet)

For the connection over Craig Ysgafn to Moelwyn Bach, continue from the summit in an east-south-east direction, following a line of small standing stones (but take care, there is another line of stones leading down to the head of Cwm Croesor), and as the ground steepens turn south to pick up the connecting ridge.

For Moelwyn Bach start from Croesor crossroads as for Moelwyn Mawr, but continue beyond Pont Maesgwm to climb to a small area of forest. Pass through gates, and shortly after leaving the forest a track bears left. Take this, and almost immediately go left again on a much fainter path ascending the west ridge of Moelwyn Bach. This path later divides, the left fork going to Bwlch Stwlan between the two Moelwyns. The right fork continues up the hill to the summit cairn.

DISTANCE: 4 kilometres (2.5 miles)
ASCENT: 555 metres (1820 feet)

To continue northwards to Moelwyn Mawr, start by descending south of east to find a standing stone which leads to a slate path across Moelwyn Bach's north-east face. The upper part of this path is loose, and the whole of it dubious under snow and ice conditions, but otherwise it leads directly to Bwlch Stwlan. A retrospective view from Bwlch Stwlan will reveal the enormous overhanging, gashed crag on Moelwyn Bach's north face – reason enough not to come down that way.

Route 5.3 Cnicht from Croesor Cnicht is one of the more popular summits of Wales, and deservedly so, being of just the right height and distance for an easy day's walking. It has, too, the advantage of being an excellent viewpoint.

Start from the car park in the once-busy village of Croesor (631446), and take the road north-west over the nearby stream. This climbs for a short distance, and then descends slightly to a stile beyond which lies a rough track. Follow the track for a while until a way-marking post points to the open hillside, and continue on a fairly clear track on to the lower end of the south-west ridge. The summit of Cnicht remains in view throughout most of the ascent as the ridge rises gradually, only finally disappearing from sight near the top where a bit of scrambling becomes necessary. The top is a narrow, rocky point adorned by a small cairn.

DISTANCE: 3 kilometres (1.9 miles)
ASCENT: 535 metres (1755 feet)

It makes a nice circular walk to continue along the ridge of Cnicht, taking care particularly in mist to keep on the path. There is a distinct tendency in poor visibility to move to the right, and to start descending to the top of Cwm Croesor far too soon. Make instead for Llyn yr Adar, and, keeping it on your left, continue to a large cairn at 657478 where a path (shown on the map) intersects the district boundary. Follow this path, narrow but clear, to Llyn Cwm Corsiog, and from there to the ruins of the Rhosydd Quarry, which ceased working in the 1920s. The quarry is a fascinating place, and is worth a little of your time.

From the quarry move west to gain a track descending into Cwm Croesor, taking, for preference, the path descending across the flanks of Moelwyn Mawr rather than that through the valley bottom.

Route 5.4 Ysgafell Wen and the Dog Lakes from Nanmor Ysgafell Wen is more a rising ridge than a summit of any distinction. The ridge forms the upper boundary of Cwm Fynhadog Uchaf (not named on the 1:50 000 map), south-west of Moel Siabod. The whole area is rough and wild, but a delightful change from well-beaten paths and crowds. There are in fact two summits, neither of which is clearly named on the 1:50 000 map. The northerly summit, the lower of the two and unnamed, is marked by a spot height, 668, though the latest height given by the Ordnance Survey is one metre higher. The higher summit lies at the meeting of the district boundaries.

The ascent, from the upper part of the Nanmor valley, is pleasant enough, and starts at the converted chapel, Blaen Nant (635491 – not named). Start through a gate opposite Blaen Nant, and descend a short distance to farm buildings. Keep these on the right, and cross a stretch of wet ground to another building over to the left. Pass around the building and then pick up a reasonable path climbing to the almost circular Llyn Llagi, hiding beneath steep broken cliffs.

Continue past the lake, and up the obvious gully ahead, from the top of which it is possible to follow a faint path, right, to Llyn yr Adar. From Llyn yr Adar it is only a short uphill walk to the top of Ysgafell Wen.

Alternatively, from the top of the gully continue ahead in a straight line to Llynnau'r Cwn, *Dog Lakes* – a group of three small lakes immediately below the unnamed summit north of Ysgafell Wen, which is then easily attainable.
DISTANCE: 3.5 kilometres (2.2 miles)
ASCENT: 495 metres (1620 feet)

This easy little walk can usefully be combined with Route 5.5 to form an enjoyable circuit of these seldom visited hills.

Route 5.5 Moel Meirch from Nantgwynant The area around Moel Meirch on the southern side of Nantgwynant is one of wild and rugged beauty. The ground dips and twists endlessly, and large knuckles of rock project everywhere. It is an excellent training ground for map reading.

Start from the car park adjoining the Bethania Bridge and leave the A498 at 626503 along a minor road which crosses the river and ascends gradually through pleasant countryside, leading eventually into the seclusion of the Nanmor valley. Follow this road until, at a sharp right turn, it is possible to take a descending farm track to Hafodydd Brithion (640494). Do not be misled by the footpath signpost at the bend in the road.

Along the path to Hafodydd Brithion the way is sign-posted 'Llyn Edno' and passes through a conspicuous rocky gorge down which tumbles the Afon Llynedno. Pass through the gorge, sometimes difficult when the stream is in spate, and cross the stream near the top. Moel Meirch is the summit on the left skyline, opposite an array of rock pinnacles which guard Llyn Edno. Pass beneath the pinnacles and ascend to the watershed where you encounter an old iron fence-line. Here go left and, leaving the fence, ascend to the rocky top of Moel Meirch.

DISTANCE: 5 kilometres (3.1 miles)
ASCENT: 545 metres (1790 feet)

To return to the fence-line and follow it around lonely Llyn Edno will eventually take you on to the two summits of Ysgafell Wen, from where you can reverse Route 5.4 to return to the Nanmor valley.

The two Moelwyns from the south-west.

Route 5.6 Allt Fawr from the Crimea Pass The eastern slopes of Allt Fawr are for ever scarred by the spoil of the Oakeley Quarries, but can be avoided by walkers who are prepared to start their day from the top of the Crimea Pass (699486), where the A470 begins to descend to Dolwyddelan.

From here it is easy to gain the long north-east ridge of Allt Fawr and follow it to the spacious summit. This approach gives extensive views across the intervening moorland of Cwm Fynhadog Uchaf to the ridge of Ysgafell Wen, and the Snowdon group beyond.

DISTANCE: 2.5 kilometres (1.6 miles)
ASCENT: 315 metres (1030 feet)

The continuation west from Allt Fawr's two rocky summits (the northerly one is the higher) to Moel Druman is pleasurable and easy, and leads into an area of lakes which constantly reflect the changing moods of the weather.

The overhanging crag on Moelwyn Bach seen from the summit of Craig Ysgafn.

Route 5.7 Moel yr Hydd by Cwmorthin Moel yr Hydd, *Hill of the Stag*, is surrounded by industrial dereliction, but it still manages to retain some dignity, and is well worth visiting. It rises above the slate-grey town of Blaenau Ffestiniog, in an area understandably left out of the Snowdonia National Park. Modern interest in industrial archaeology is such, however, that it may only be a matter of time before this dismal area becomes a major tourist attraction, rather than the minor one it is now.

The most interesting way to Moel yr Hydd is from Tanygrisiau (687451), through Cwmorthin, which, of all the wild and wonderful places traveller and antiquarian Thomas Pennant visited in Wales in the eighteenth century, he singled out as especially attractive. All that was changed in the next century when man made his violent impact, burrowing slate veins deep inside Moelwyn Mawr and Moel yr Hydd. Enormous tips of slate waste spilled out onto the hillsides, and everywhere saw the commotion of men, machines, railways, dams and reservoirs. But all that is long finished, and now nature is trying hard to take back the gaunt, grey remnants of a by-gone age.

From Tanygrisiau take the road from the post office leading under the nearby railway bridge, and climb along the quarry track into Cwmorthin. This is an enormous valley, with cliffs and industrial scars high on both sides. In its midst stand abandoned houses, a derelict chapel, and a desolate, lily-garlanded lake. Follow the quarry track as it climbs through more spoil to the wide plateau separating Cwmorthin from Cwm Croesor, on which stand the remains of the Rhosydd Quarry. Just beyond the main surviving buildings a cold, dripping level entrance can be found, sending its chill draught out into the air. Climb behind the entrance on to a ramp, and at the top of the ramp go left across broken ground towards Moel yr Hydd. The neat summit is a surprising viewpoint.

DISTANCE: 4 kilometres (2.5 miles)
ASCENT: 465 metres (1525 feet)

Mists close in around the summit of Craig Ysgafn.

Route 5.8 Moel Penamnen from the Crimea Pass Moel Penamnen, overlooking the slate town of Blaenau Ffestiniog, is in the wrong place to satisfy any search for beauty or pastoral reflection. But walkers with only half a day to spare will find a reward in tranquillity.

Start from 698484 just below the top of the Crimea Pass on the A470, and take a shepherds' track to the two lakes, Llynnau Barlwyd, from where it is easy to gain the ridge north of Moel Penamnen. Follow the ridge south to the small summit.
DISTANCE: 2.5 kilometres (1.6 miles)
ASCENT: 240 metres (790 feet)

A return over the minor top, Moel Farlwyd, would not go amiss.

Route 5.9 Manod Mawr Manod Mawr lies a few kilometres north-east of Ffestiniog, and is an infrequently visited hill, though unjustly so. A beautiful lake separates it from its near and lower neighbour, Manod Bach, and such intrusion as there is of man's industry is less noticeable than among the hills around Blaenau Ffestiniog a short distance to the north. What aren't noticeable are the vast caverns of Manod, created by slate mining and protected by a government cloak of secrecy. Labyrinthine tunnels and cathedral-like vaults riddle the heart of the mountain, and during the war were used to store treasures from the National Gallery.

Start along the minor road running south-east from the junction of the A470 and A496 at 705444. Pass some cottages, and, after a gate, keep to a farm track for a short distance. Just before the farm buildings go left and cross a small stream. Follow the true left bank of the stream until, at the top of the field through which it flows, it is possible to ascend, right, by a wall into a higher pasture. Across the pasture a fence-line ascends to the vicinity of Llyn y Manod where there is a gate.

Follow a track around the east side of the lake and cross the lower slopes of Manod Mawr to the col between it and the unnamed summit to the north. From the col, appropriately named Bwlch y Slates, where there is a small lake, turn right, south, and ascend easily to the trig on Manod's summit.

DISTANCE: 3.5 kilometres (2.2 miles)
ASCENT: 445 metres (1460 feet)

Section 6 – Rhinogs

	MAP REFERENCE	HEIGHT (m)	1:50 000 OS MAP
Y Llethr	661258	756	124
Diffwys	661234	750	124
Rhinog Fawr	657290	720	124
Rhinog Fach	665270	712	124
Y Garn	702230	629	124
Moel Ysgafarnogod	658346	623	124

From the Mawddach estuary in the south, the Rhinog range pushes its way northwards to the Vale of Ffestiniog through 24 kilometres (15 miles) of the most uncompromising and roughest country in the whole of Wales. The hard Cambrian grits, brought to the surface by an upfold of the rock strata known as the Harlech Dome, favour the growth of heather above all else and, with the profusion of huge boulders partly buried in peat, give the whole area an appealing rugged splendour.

But not everyone shares my view of this amazing landscape of boggy hollows, bare rock precipices and knobbly ridge crests, liberally dappled with lonely lakes. Thomas Pennant in his *Tour in Wales* said of Bwlch Drws Ardudwy, one of only two practical crossings of the range: "I was tempted to visit this noted pass, and found the horror of it far exceeding the most gloomy idea that could be conceived of it. The sides seemed to have been rent by some mighty convulsion into a thousand precipices . . ." The Reverend W. Bingley a few years later found it "a place well calculated to inspire a timid mind with terror". Black's *Picturesque Guide to North Wales* claims that "Nothing can exceed the dreariness and desolation of this ravine, overshadowed by the rugged, frowning cliffs of Rhinog Fawr and Rhinog Fach." While Patrick Monkhouse, writing in the early 1930s of Rhinog Fawr, in his own inimitable style claimed that the mountain "exacted more perspiration to the yard than any other . . . in Wales, with the possible exception of the other side of the same mountain". Not exactly what you would call an encouraging introduction; yet it is only one side of the true picture.

The Rhinogs are fascinating, rewarding country.

The northern end of the range rises to a flattish ridge where the bare rock, cracked and broken like the mud of a dried pond, thrusts through the heather. And everywhere the light catches the eyes of numerous small, clear lakes – Llyn Caerwych, Llyn y Fedw, Llyn Pryfed and many more. Further south, on either side of Rhinog Fawr, are the only two ways across the range, the notorious Bwlch Drws Ardudwy, and to the north, Bwlch Tyddiad, renowned for its 'Roman' Steps, though there is little evidence to show that the Romans were ever interested in the coastal lands of Dyffryn Ardudwy. South again, beyond Rhinog Fach, lies Llyn Hywel, claimed by Gerald of Wales to contain monocular fish, and into which plunge steep, bare rocky slabs planed so smooth that they might have seen the passage of glaciers only this century instead of 10 000 years ago.

Y Llethr, the highest summit, and Diffwys display contrasting sides. On the west smooth grassland rolls down to the sea, while on the east they revert to type as you struggle through ankle-twisting heather-covered rocks to Y Garn.

Perhaps the image is one of ruggedness and bleakness, but there are ways through, and the walker who ventures here will be rewarded far more for his effort than anywhere else in Wales.

Route 6.1 Moel Ysgafarnogod The whole northern section of the Rhinog range is some of the most testing walking to be found anywhere in Britain, compelling lowly Moel Ysgafarnogod to become one of the most challenging hills in the country.

A fair acceptance of this challenge would start at 654396 on the A496, along a minor road. Leave the road at 666393 to follow a path leading first to Rhaeadr Du, *Black Falls*, and then to the shores of Llyn Trawsfynydd from where the twisting north ridge of Moel Ysgafarnogod may be gained and pursued over Diffwys (not to be confused with

the higher summit further south) and Foel Penolau to the summit trig.
DISTANCE: 8 kilometres (5 miles)
ASCENT: 615 metres (2020 feet)

An alternative approach from the south is via Cwm Bychan. A way-marked path (white arrows) ascends from the lake (643315) diagonally across the southern slopes of Clip, from where it is possible to gain the main ridge and continue north to Ysgafarnogod. Another pearl of a walk!
DISTANCE: 3.5 kilometres (2.2 miles)
ASCENT: 455 metres (1490 feet)

Route 6.2 Rhinog Fawr by Cwm Bychan and the Roman Steps One might reasonably expect Rhinog Fawr to be the highest of the Rhinog range, but that distinction is reserved for Y Llethr. However, looking at the range from the east, it is easy to see why Rhinog Fawr appeared so formidable.

At the end of Cwm Bychan stands a farm (648314) once occupied by Ieuan Llwyd who claimed lineal descent from Welsh lords living in this region as far back as 1100. Just before the farm there is a large car park-cum-camp-site, and from it a signposted track heads roughly southwards, climbing first through woodland, and then entering a narrow gorge leading to the summit of the pass, Bwlch Tyddiad. Of the two breaks in the Rhinog range, Bwlch Tyddiad is rather better known, though less obvious, for along its approach from Cwm Bychan hundreds of large slabs of gritstone have been laid to make a well-defined track, known as the Roman Steps. This paved way, however, is more likely to be of early medieval date, possibly constructed when Edward I rebuilt Harlech castle. As an inland route, traversing beyond the Rhinogs' open moorland country eastwards to the Dee trench at Bala, this crossing was important not only politically – Pennant comments on the dependency of Bala on the castle at Harlech – but also as a trade route for wool and other merchandise between Bala and the coastland.

The ascent by the Roman Steps to Bwlch Tyddiad is as enjoyable a route as any in the Rhinogs, but from the top of the pass the going gets rough. For the 'simplest' line, continue beyond the top of the pass for about 40 metres, and then climb steeply, right, up a gully filled with boulders, keeping right, near the top, to emerge on a rocky knoll north of Llyn Du. The way across the knoll is marked by small cairns. West of Llyn Du a wall then delineates the next part of the route as it climbs to a point almost due west of Rhinog Fawr's summit. From here make directly for Rhinog Fawr (east), and ascend a short scree slope (which can be avoided easily enough). Once above the scree follow a clear path to the summit trig and cairns.

DISTANCE: 3.25 kilometres (2 miles)

ASCENT: 550 metres (1805 feet)

The Rhinog range from the east, in which Rhinog Fawr appears much higher than the highest summit of the range, Y Llethr, two mountains to the left.

Return the way you came is always good advice in the Rhinogs, though the wall encountered west of Llyn Du continues north, descending very steeply to Bwlch Tyddiad to meet the Steps a short distance west of the top of the pass. This option can of course be used in ascent, but is very tiring.

There is an alternative, very rough, descent from Llyn Du to the larger lake, Gloywlyn, but this is virtually trackless until an anglers' path is met leading from the north-east shore of the lake back to the valley. Don't go this way if you are already tired and weary!

Route 6.3 Rhinog Fawr and Rhinog Fach by Bwlch Drws Ardudwy The ascent to Bwlch Drws Ardudwy, from where either of the Rhinogs may be reached, starts from the roadhead of Cwm Nantcol at Maes y Garnedd (642269), where, for a fee, cars may be parked. This farm

Sombre Llyn Hywel, the haunt of monocular fish, lies beneath the scree slopes of Rhinog Fach.

was the birthplace of John Jones the Regicide, a colonel in Cromwell's army, who married Cromwell's sister and, in signing the death warrant of Charles I, committed the crime for which he was to be hanged, drawn and quartered in 1660.

The start of the path to Bwlch Drws Ardudwy is signposted at Maes y Garnedd, and the route fairly obvious, with the mountains growing ever larger as you near the top of the pass. Some of the gritstone slabs found in Cwm Bychan recur along this route, though with less prominence.

The top of the pass is marked by a large cairn. Here turn left, north, for Rhinog Fawr along a faint path leading to a wall through the base of which there is a large hole. An undignified scramble through the hole is preferable to an undignified and unnecessary clambering over the wall with its attendant risk of damage. Beyond the wall, follow a sketchy path to the summit, along which I once encountered a large herd of feral goats. Do not be tempted into trying to leave such path as there is; you would only head into sweaty and exhausting trouble.

DISTANCE: 4 kilometres (2.5 miles)
ASCENT: 535 metres (1755 feet)

From the cairn at the pass turn right, south, for Rhinog Fach and climb very steeply for half an hour. This is unremitting toil that only eases when the northern end of the summit ridge is reached, but the view from there on a good day is tremendous.

DISTANCE: 4 kilometres (2.5 miles)
ASCENT: 530 metres (1740 feet)

Do not be tempted to descend south directly from the summit of Rhinog Fach; this leads to a steep, brutal scree slope falling to Llyn Hywel. It is better to side-track a little to reach a wall descending to the vicinity of Llyn Hywel.

To continue to Y Llethr follow the wall to the bwlch between the two mountains, and then ascend, still with the wall, in a series of rocky steps, pausing to look back at the amazing tilted slabs that fall into Llyn Hywel, until you reach the unexpectedly grassy summit plateau. Alternatively, you can take a more obvious line up the wide gully to the right of the wall, which will afford photographers with a better view of the two Rhinogs.

To descend to Cwm Nantcol, head west of south for the stile just below the summit of Y Llethr, keeping the wall on the left, and descend open moorland, parallel to a wall and later crossing a new fence by a stile, until a bulldozed track is reached which leads to Cil Cychwyn (634259) in the valley.

Route 6.4 Y Llethr from Tal y Bont A long, gentle approach to the highest summit of the Rhinog range can be made from the village of Tal y Bont on the A496 north of Barmouth. Start at a car park near some toilets and a telephone box adjoining the main road from where a narrow lane follows the bubbling Afon Ysgethin through pleasant woodland to a cottage, Lletty-lloegr (606226 – not named on the 1:50000 map), near Pont Fadog. The cottage may also be reached by road by leaving the A496 at 586224, and following a minor road. But watch for the right turn through a gate near Cors y Gedol.

Go to the rear of Lletty-lloegr and follow the first wall you encounter upwards through bracken and gorse to a stone stile (not obvious) through another wall, this time bounding a wide track. Follow this track until open countryside is reached, with the rounded dome of Moelfre rising on your left. The track makes ultimately for Llyn Bodlyn beneath the broken cliffs of Diffwys, but should be left long before the lake to make a rising traverse to the low col between Moelfre and Y Llethr where another wall will be met. Follow this wall to the stile just below the summit of Y Llethr, from where it is an easy, short pull to the summit.

DISTANCE: 9 kilometres (5.6 miles)
ASCENT: 725 metres (2380 feet)

The long wall ascending to the summit of Y Llethr is a sure guide in misty conditions.

The wall on Y Llethr continues unbroken across the summit of the minor top, Crib y Rhiw.

The highest point of Crib y Rhiw, the connecting ridge between Y Llethr and Diffwys.

The summit of Diffwys.

Continuation to Diffwys, across the minor top, Crib y Rhiw, also requires a return to the stile, this time to cross it and follow the undulations of Crib y Rhiw to a conspicuous path climbing to the summit. There is a wall across the whole of this section which can be followed safely in mist, though it avoids the conspicuous path, which in any event seems a pointless short cut.

Route 6.5 Diffwys from Tal y Bont Follow Route 6.4 to Lletty-lloegr, but instead of going to the rear of the cottage, descend, right, on a track to Pont Fadog, and then follow a clear track (later deteriorating into a path) to the vicinity of Pont Scethin. En route you will pass Llyn Irddyn, a secluded lake that is unnoticed until you are almost on top of it. Near Pont Scethin you join the old Harlech track once used on the journey from London to Harlech. Here turn right and ascend by the track to the Llawlech ridge, and there turn left to follow a wall to the summit of Diffwys.
DISTANCE: 9.5 kilometres (6 miles)
ASCENT: 720 metres (2360 feet)

By reversing Route 6.5 and combining it with Route 6.4 to Y Llethr you can undertake the finest excursion in the Rhinogs. And all of it free from heather and boulders and broken rocks!

Route 6.6 Y Garn Y Garn is something of a loner among the Rhinogs, being separated from the rest by the valley of the Afon Cwm-mynach, but it is a summit which will please lovers of the rough Rhinog country. To add to the interest, "Thar's gold in them thar hills", for the southern part of the range, overlooking the Mawddawch estuary, has seen quite a number of gold mines in its time, with one at least, Clogau St David's, on the west of the valley, being re-opened in recent years.

The Roman Steps in Cwm Bychan, leading to Bwlch Tyddiad. ▶

Start into Cwm Mynarch – *Monk's Valley*, a memory of Cymer Abbey – until a metalled track, signposted (689200), leads towards Cesailgwm-bach (697213). After a while this track descends, right, to cross a stream, and is here signposted 'New Precipice Walk'. From the bridge stay with the track (and the New Precipice Walk) until it is possible to gain Foel Ispri (another gold mine site), and from there the long south ridge of Y Garn. This route is, however, a little circuitous and can be short-circuited by going left from the top of the rise just after the bridge along a rough track towards Cesailgwm-bach. By keeping the farm below and on the left a pathless ascent can later be made, diagonally upwards to the right, to the south ridge. This is quite rough, but gives a lovely insight into the head of the cwm below Y Garn.

The wall along the south ridge needs to be crossed at a gap, and then later re-crossed at a gate not far from the small lake, Nannau-is-afon. All this crossing of walls puts the lake out of sight, but from it there remains only a short pull to the summit.

DISTANCE: 5 kilometres (3.1 miles)
ASCENT: 625 metres (2050 feet)

Walkers wanting a longer return, who do not mind rough going, should continue north-west from the top of Y Garn to join the edge of the forest shown on the map. There is a faint path leading along the forest boundary to the track at 681244 from where a very pleasant return can be made through Cwm Mynarch. Much of the ground north and north-west of Y Garn is completely wild and trackless, and in the event of bad weather help is a long way away.

Section 7 – Arenigs

	MAP REFERENCE	HEIGHT (m)	1:50000 OS MAP
Arenig Fawr	827369	854	124/125
Moel Llyfnant	808352	751	124/125

Rhobell Fawr	787257	734	124
Arenig Fach	821416	689	124/125
Carnedd y Filiast	871446	669	124/125
Dduallt	811274	662	124/125
Carnedd Llechwedd Llyfn	857446	643	124/125
Foel Boeth	779345	619	124
Foel Goch	953423	611	125

ROUTES
7.1 Arenig Fawr by Llyn Arenig Fawr
7.2 Moel Llyfnant from Pont Rhyd y Fen
7.3 Rhobell Fawr from Rhydymain
7.4 Dduallt from Rhydymain

In grouping this particular collection of mountain summits under the heading Arenigs I have perhaps been more arbitrary than elsewhere. The whole area is vast with four distinct groups of hills: the highest centring on the two Arenigs, Fawr and Fach, while further south rise Rhobell Fawr and Dduallt. North-east of Arenig Fach, and with its southern boundaries delineated by Llyn Celyn, a small group of moorland hills gathers around Carnedd y Filiast. Further east still lies one of numerous Foel Gochs in Wales, an isolated hill of little interest.

The two Arenigs have much in common, their profiles dominating the moorland landscape from which they rise. They both have considerable bulk of hard igneous rocks that have endured where other, softer rocks have been eroded away; and they have along their eastern aspects an array of cliffs falling into beautiful lakes.

Between Arenig Fawr and the more northerly Arenig Fach flows the Afon Tryweryn, dammed during the early 1960s to provide a reservoir for Liverpool, and consuming in the process the village of Capel Celyn. Here, however, the despoliation is perhaps less intrusive than in other parts of Wales, and there is an almost natural attractiveness about Llyn Celyn now.

North-west of Arenig Fach, and south-west of Arenig Fawr (and its attendant Moel Llyfnant), the land is one of

Dduallt, Black Height, *rises above afforested land beyond Ty Newydd y Mynydd.*

Llyn Arenig Fawr beneath the north-eastern crags of Arenig Fawr.

Arenig Fawr rises above the moorland in the beautiful Lliw valley.

The twin summits of Arenig Fawr are a familiar landmark from the east.

wild, untroubled bogland. Indeed the land north-west of Arenig Fach is known as the Migneint, meaning bogland. But it has a special appeal for walkers with the time to meander across its vastness, and is worthy of exploration.

To the south the two summits, Rhobell Fawr and Dduallt, may both be ascended easily from Rhydymain, and provide rewarding alternatives to more popular routes in the Arans or around Cader Idris.

Route 7.1 Arenig Fawr by Llyn Arenig Fawr Undoubtedly the most satisfying ascent of Arenig Fawr is that which takes a rising grassy path leaving the old Bala–Ffestiniog road 2.5 kilometres (1.6 miles) east of Pont Rhyd y Fen, at 845395.

Follow the path until it reaches Llyn Arenig Fawr, with the cliffs of the mountain rising abruptly on the right in a truly wild setting. Continue, left, around the lake to the dam at its outflow which can usually be crossed without too much difficulty, though the outflow itself needs to be crossed by means of a short section of iron ladder conveniently placed nearby.

Once across the dam a faint path ascends the ridge rising above the southern shore of the lake. The summit appears on the left, and is easily reached by continuing up the ridge until it meets the main axis of the mountain (an elongated, undulating north–south ridge) along the greater part of which there is a fence. The fence-line passes close by the actual summit, which is marked by a stone shelter bearing a memorial stone to the crash there in 1943 of an American Flying Fortress with the loss of all six crewmen.

DISTANCE: 4.5 kilometres (2.8 miles)
ASCENT: 525 metres (1720 feet)

There is an easy descent south over the minor tops of Carreg y Diocyn and Craig y Bychan, before a further descent, west, leads to the col with Moel Llyfnant. A return to Pont Rhyd y Fen may then be made by reversing Route 7.2.

Route 7.2 Moel Llyfnant from Pont Rhyd y Fen This is not the shortest or most direct ascent of Moel Llyfnant, but it is the most pleasant. There is a short stretch of bog-bashing, but nothing to deter the dedicated walker bent on solitude and good views amid wild country.

From the vicinity of Pont Rhyd y Fen go west along the track which parallels the course of the old railway. After one kilometre (0.6 miles) this abandons the railway and heads south to the derelict, but beautifully placed, Amnodd Wen (816375). Continue south from Amnodd Wen along a sketchy path, above the line of the forest, to the marshy col between Arenig Fawr and Moel Llyfnant. From the col ascend west across trackless ground to the summit of Moel Llyfnant, overlooking the Lliw valley, a pass once used by the Romans during their invasion of this area.

DISTANCE: 5.5 kilometres (3.4 miles)
ASCENT: 385 metres (1265 feet)

Route 7.3 Rhobell Fawr from Rhydymain This 'noble mountain', as Patrick Monkhouse described it, is ideal for a short day, or, combined with its neighbour, Dduallt, turns into a fuller excursion. The intervening land between the two mountains is, however, now newly afforested, and though passage is feasible (see Route 7.4 for details) it calls for some ingenuity.

By far the easiest ascent is from the south, leaving the A494 at 799216 and pursuing a minor road followed by forest tracks all the way to Ty Newydd y Mynydd, now in ruins. It is not advisable to take cars the whole way to Ty Newydd, since there is nowhere to park them when you get there. In any event to do so significantly detracts from the pleasure of a gradual ascent through forest plantations with the noble mountain growing ever larger on the left.

At Ty Newydd y Mynydd take a gate on the opposite side of the track, and then cross a small ridge and a boggy depression. The eastern slopes of Rhobell Fawr lie ahead, and can be ascended without difficulty. In mist follow a

wall to the rocky summit plateau, but it does not continue to the actual summit, on which there is a trig point and a cairn.

DISTANCE: From the A494: 6 kilometres (3.75 miles)
ASCENT: 615 metres (2015 feet)

Route 7.4 Dduallt from Rhydymain The Black Height has long been an interesting mountain to climb, but getting on to it is now proving difficult because of forest plantations. If you are not averse to quiet contemplation as you plod across sometimes awkward terrain, Dduallt is well worth the effort. The views from the summit are extensive, and the mountain is sufficiently distant from its higher neighbour, Rhobell Fawr, not to be dominated by it.

◀ *The rugged shape of Moel Llyfnant, seen from the Lliw valley.*

Craig y Bychan, in the distance, is the southern end of the long ridge of Arenig Fawr, and feeds the waters of the Afon Erwent flowing here through a narrow gorge to join the Afon Lliw. ▼

Follow Route 7.3 to Ty Newydd y Mynydd where you will see the space shown on the 1:50 000 map now filled with young trees. Continue along the forest track until you reach the edge of the older, northerly forest at 800264, and here turn right, off the track, to follow a minor path along the forest boundary. This, in reality, is now a fire break between the old and new forests.

At 806259 you reach a small knoll, not apparent on the map, from where you should make directly for the southern end of the Dduallt ridge. The intervening land is boggy and tussocky with minor rock outcrops, making navigation in mist difficult, but the ascent of the ridge, when it is reached, is one of the pleasures of the Welsh mountains. Towards the top of the ridge you encounter a fence which leads to within a few metres of the summit, marked by a neat cairn on top of a small outcrop.

DISTANCE: 8 kilometres (5 miles)
ASCENT: 540 metres (1770 feet)

Section 8 – Cader Idris, Dovey and Tarren Hills

	MAP REFERENCE	HEIGHT (m)	1:50 000 OS MAP
Cader Idris			
Pen y Gadair			
(Cader Idris)	711130	893	124
Mynydd Moel	727137	863	124
Cyfrwy	704133	811	124
Mynydd Pencoed	711121	791	124
Gau Craig	744141	683	124
Tyrau Mawr	677135	661	124
Craig y Llyn	665119	622	124
Dovey			
Maesglasau	823152	674	124/125
Waun Oer	786148	670	124
Cribin Fawr	795153	659	124
Mynydd Ceiswyn	772139	604	124
Mynydd Dolgoed	802142	604	124/125

Tarren Hills

Tarren y Gesail	711059	667	124
Tarrenhendre	683041	634	135

The distinctive character of the Cader Idris range derives from the way ice has gouged great corrie basins into the volcanic rocks with impressive results. It is the sheer scale of erosion which attracts people to the range, often in preference to the higher mountains further north in Snowdonia, and understandably so. One such corrie basin, in which reposes Llyn y Gadair, is the legendary Chair of Idris, from which the range takes its name. Idris, in some accounts, is a mythical giant; in others he is a local worthy given to much contemplation amid the summits, while yet other tales recount him as someone killed in battle against the Saxons in 630. Belief in the existence of elves or fairies in the caves of Cader Idris is still widely held. But they are good spirits, despite the often malevolent and grim aspect of the mountain.

The whole area has long been popular with tourists. For over fifty years in the eighteenth century Robin Edwards of Dolgellau guided clients across the Cader Idris range, while the arrival of the Cambrian Railway at Barmouth in the mid-nineteenth century opened up the countryside to a new wave of Victorian excursionists. Even as recently as the beginning of this century guides advertised their services in Dolgellau to take visitors up the mountain.

Victorian commercial initiative was also responsible for

another of the features of Cader Idris, the remains of a stone refreshment hut on its highest summit, Pen y Gadair, where, according to a contemporary writer, visitors could partake of refreshments "while waiting the dispersion of the misty clouds in order to enjoy the exquisite prospect". The clouds are often still there, but the refreshments are not.

Dolgellau, dominated by the vastness of the Cader Idris range, is an ancient market town in a wide and fertile valley through which flows the river Wnion. Roman roads meet here, and in 1404, Owain Glyndŵr (a descendant through his mother of the last native Prince of Wales, Llywelyn the Great) assembled the last Welsh Parliament here, from which Glyndŵr issued letters patent in sovereign style appointing ambassadors to go to France to sign a treaty of alliance with Charles IV against the English. The house in which the Parliament sat, incidentally, was taken down in 1882, to make room for a shop, and was removed in its entirety to Newtown, where it now stands in Sir Pryce Jones' Park.

Route 8.1 Pen y Gadair from Ty Nant Ty Nant farm (697152) lies about 4.5 kilometres (3 miles) south-west of Dolgellau. It is not identified on the 1:50 000 map, but the nearby National Park car park and toilets are. Considering that the ascent to the whole Cader Idris ridge involves tackling the steep escarpment which is its most noble feature, the effort involved is surprisingly less than might be anticipated. This is largely due to pathway reconstruction works which now ease the worst of the gradient and circumvent the most eroded spots.

Turn right from the car park and cross the road bridge to a signposted track on the left, adjoining a telephone box. This leads to Ty Nant farm from where the way through the lower fields is way-marked and very pleasant. Later the path climbs to the foot of the escarpment, where it starts zig-zagging to avoid badly eroded stretches before reaching the shoulder of the long ridge connecting Pen y

Gadair with Tyrau Mawr at Rhiw Gwredydd. A line of standing stones (useful markers in descent) leads to two stiles; cross the first, but ignore the second. Instead turn left along a wide, peaty path, later becoming a rocky track, and leading to Pen y Gadair 2 kilometres (1.25 miles) distant. The summit is marked by a trig point, and has a stone shelter nearby.

DISTANCE: 3.75 kilometres (2.3 miles)
ASCENT: 745 metres (2445 feet)

Route 8.2 Llyn y Gadair by Fox's Path Despite its inclusion here this once very popular way to Cader Idris is now so badly eroded in its upper reaches as to be positively dangerous. The whole top section is loose, unstable scree at a very steep angle, and slides at the slightest provocation; it needs fencing off and leaving alone for twenty or so years. Fox's Path (sometimes Foxes Path) is however a really superb approach walk, and well worth pursuing as far as Llyn y Gadair, but please go no further. The distances and ascents given below extend only to Llyn y Gadair.

For convenience, start from the Ty Nant car park (697152), and walk back along the road to just beyond Llyn Gwernan, where the path is signposted. The path is clear throughout, with only one short stretch of wet ground, and climbs first to Llyn y Gafr before ascending again to Llyn y Gadair.

The immense bulk of Pen y Gadair and its satellite, Cyfrwy, which together make Cader Idris, *Chair of Idris*, dominate the view ahead, almost, in the vicinity of the upper lake, wrapping themselves around you. The feel of the mountain environment is very real here, water splashes and gurgles all around, gulls and ravens vie for air space, and scree rattles endlessly downward. Yet for all that, there is a tremendous feeling of peace and satisfaction; don't spoil it by attempting the scree slope!

DISTANCE: 3.5 kilometres (2.2 miles)
ASCENT: 400 metres (1310 feet)

The steep, broken northern escarpment of Cader Idris viewed from Cyfrwy. The summit on the right is Pen y Gadair, and in the distance, on the left, Mynydd Moel.

Llyn Cau, Enclosed Lake, *beneath the steep cliffs of Mynydd Pencoed.*

The Great Gully, Mynydd Pencoed. ▶

The Minffordd Path into Cwm Cau, with Mynydd Pencoed at the head of ▶▶ the cwm, and Pen y Gadair rising on the right.

Route 8.3 Pen y Gadair and Mynydd Pencoed from Minffordd This is a fine mountaineering route, possessing all the attributes of ruggedness, beauty and extensive scenery. Were it not for the comparative remoteness of Minffordd as a starting point, and the problems of parking when you get there, it would be the most popular route up the mountain. As it is, it is not without its supporters, necessitating Nature Conservancy repair work in the lower sections.

The ascent starts through the wrought-iron gates of the old Idris Estate at Minffordd (730114), and passes through ancient oak woods and up into the enclosed hollow containing Llyn Cau, behind which the cliffs of the Mynydd Pencoed rise almost vertically. The way is seldom in doubt, but walkers intending to complete a circular walk by taking in Mynydd Moel would do well on leaving the woods behind to read the lie of the land descending from Mynydd Moel to the woods, by which way you will return later in the day.

Once in Cwm Cau it is worth diverting from the main path to visit the lake where, as I once did, you can comfortably fall asleep and forget all about the heights above! Less indolent walkers should return to the main path and continue up a short scree track ascending the southern wall of the cwm to a fine ridge overlooking Cwm Amarch and the Dysynni valley. The ridge affords superb views into both cwms – especially from the top of the Great Gully of Mynydd Pencoed – and across the Dysynni to the Tarren Hills.

The way over Mynydd Pencoed is easy enough, but on reaching the summit walkers who have even the least degree of vertigo are advised not to approach too close to the edge of the drop into the cwm below – it's rather sudden!

From Mynydd Pencoed there is a short descent to a col, from where it is possible to descend loose scree back to the lake, followed by a final rocky pull to the summit of Pen y Gadair.

DISTANCE: 4 kilometres (2.5 miles)
ASCENT: 870 metres (2855 feet)

Route 8.4 Pen y Gadair through Cwm Pennant For comparative peace and quiet there is much to commend this route through one of the most beautiful, elongated cwms in North Wales. It is less popular than other lines of ascent, mainly because its start is remote, its way is long, and, until approaching the main Cader Idris ridge, there is little of interest. But this option facilitates an excellent return over the adjoining summits of Tyrau Mawr and Craig y Llyn (see Route 8.5).

Start from the hamlet of Llanfihangel y Pennant (672089), and follow the road leading to Tyn y Ddôl, Mary Jones' Cottage. The cottage is now in ruins, but in its centre is a monument telling of Mary Jones' 25-mile walk to Bala, barefoot, to obtain a Welsh bible from the Reverend Thomas Charles in 1800. Charles was so impressed by the girl's dedication that he gave her his last bible, and immediately turned his thoughts to forming what was to become the British and Foreign Bible Society.

From Tyn y Ddôl continue on a graded track as far as Hafotty Gwastadfryn, from where a grassy trail leads to Rhiw Gwredydd, and joins the route ascending from Ty Nant for the rest of the way to the summit.
DISTANCE: 8 kilometres (5 miles)
ASCENT: 870 metres (2855 feet)

Route 8.5 Tyrau Mawr and Craig y Llyn Tyrau Mawr and Craig y Llyn lie at the western end of the Cader Idris ridge, presenting a steep face to the north which was considered by Thomas Pennant to be "the highest rock [he] ever rode under". They are out-of-the-way places, especially welcome on a hot day when the greater heights of Pen y Gadair and Cyfrwy are thronged with walkers.

Both summits may be reached by ascending Route 8.1 from Ty Nant as far as the main Cader Idris ridge at Rhiw Gwredydd, and there turning right, over a stile, to follow a

Mynydd Pencoed, showing the Great Gully, from the summit of Pen y Gadair.

The continuation from Pen y Gadair to Mynydd Moel.

Cyfrwy: Idris' Table is about two-thirds of the way down the summit ridge on the right.

The unsuspected summit crags of Mynydd Moel.

fence passing first over the minor top, Carnedd Lwyd – really little more than a pile of rocks – and then on to Tyrau Mawr and Craig y Llyn. The fence-line is a useful guide in mist, but does not actually cross the summit of either mountain. Walkers who do not wish to retrace their steps to Ty Nant can continue from Craig y Llyn, around the head of Cwm Cyri, in which the tiny Llyn Cyri reposes like a jewelled eye, to gain the lower summit, Braich Ddu (645121), from where an easy descent leads to a minor track joining the road back to Ty Nant either at 632121 or 647133. This entails a fair march along the road, but the scenery is pleasant and relaxing – most of the year!

DISTANCE: (To Craig y Llyn) 5 kilometres (3.1 miles)
ASCENT: 630 metres (2070 feet)

An alternative ascent may be made from the hamlet of Llanfihangel y Pennant on the Afon Cader, at the southern end of Cwm Pennant. This way follows Route 8.4 to Rhiw Gwredydd where it joins the path from Ty Nant, and follows the fence-line described above. From the summit of Craig y Llyn, however, a descent should be made back into Cwm Pennant, reaching it in the vicinity of Hafotty Gwastadfryn, by means of a new and very obvious track. This is an extremely pleasant walk, rather more away from it all than other walks in this popular area.

DISTANCE: (Round trip) 13.5 kilometres (8.4 miles)
ASCENT: 755 metres (2480 feet)

Before leaving Craig y Llyn, a short walk further to reach the secondary top reveals a curious circular mound of stones, Twll yr Ogof, but do not be tempted into trying to descend over Mynydd Pennant back to Cwm Pennant from here. I did! It's very rough, very steep and very tiring. Opt for the safe route to Hafotty Gwastadfryn.

Route 8.6 Mynydd Moel Mynydd Moel and the long ridge extending eastwards to the abrupt cliffs of Gau Craig are probably better known than all the other summits of the Cader Idris range because of their prominence in the view as you travel down the valley from Bala. Often, I suspect, Mynydd Moel is mistaken for Pen y Gadair itself, which is less conspicuous and lies further back.

For a direct ascent to Mynydd Moel, take Route 8.3 from Minffordd until you leave the woodland. Then, as soon as possible, cross the bubbling Nant Cader (not named on the 1:50000 map) as it cascades to join the Afon Dysynni below, and gain a grassy ramp running along the edge of the woodland. This soon leads to open, bracken-clad hillside and a dilapidated wall climbing towards Mynydd Moel, from where there is a fine view westward into the great hollow of Cwm Cau. The wall does not go to the summit of the mountain, but an imaginary projection of it does, in its upper reaches meeting a clear path ascending from Gau Craig to the unsuspected summit crags of Mynydd Moel.

DISTANCE: 2.5 kilometres (1.6 miles)
ASCENT: 757 metres (2485 feet)

The best way, however, of taking in Mynydd Moel is to include it in a clockwise circuit of Cwm Cau from Minffordd (described in Route 8.3 as far as Pen y Gadair). The intervening grassy ridge between Pen y Gadair and Mynydd Moel is delightful walking, especially if, instead of keeping to the path linking the two mountains, you follow the edge of the northern escarpment. There is very little re-ascent involved, and the route affords superb views northwards to the Rhinogs and beyond. Walkers then returning to Minffordd will descend by reversing the above route.

Route 8.7 The Dovey Hills To the east of the long Cader Idris ridge, across that geological shift known as the Bala Fault, lies a series of unpretentious, grassy hills forming a wholly unsuspected serpentine ridge walk that has often served me as a rewarding alternative to the more popular hills around. It does not readily lend itself to circular walks, though these can be manufactured, but responds best to a complete west-to-east traverse, ending at Dinas Mawddwy. The problems of transport to and from the beginning and end are more than compensated for along the way; in any case there is a convenient Youth Hostel just south of Dinas Mawddwy, at Minllyn, and a camp-site.

The crossing of the Dovey Hills starts from the stile at 756138, at the top of Bwlch Llyn Bach and beneath the formidable cliffs of Craig y Llam which the upheaval that created the Bala Fault has moved to their present position from the vicinity of Tal y Llyn lake some distance south-west. Ascend a shallow, slate gully on an old public footpath which later crosses to Cwm Ratgoed, and continue to a marshy plateau. Then follow the true left bank of the stream flowing into the plateau from the minor top, Mynydd y Waun, to gain the start of the ridge, at a fence and a stile, a short distance south-west of the first summit, Mynydd Ceiswyn. The ridge then ranges before you, undulating north-eastwards across Waun Oer to Cribin Fawr (the summit of which is completely unmarked), before turning south-eastwards, over Mynydd Dolgoed (more easily identified on the 1:50000 map by the cliffs on its northern face, Craig Portas), to cross a narrow grassy ridge before the final ascent to the highest summit, Maes-glasau.

The summit of Maesglasau is a large, grassy plateau with its highest point, Maen Du (on which there is a small cairn), overlooking a steep craggy drop into Cwm yr Eglwys. Continue around the rim of Craig Maesglasau to Bwlch Siglen, and then on to the minor top, Foel Dinas, before descending to forest trails in Coed Foel Dinas which lead to the Youth Hostel at Minllyn.

DISTANCE: (Complete traverse) 11.5 kilometres (7.2 miles)

ASCENT: 670 metres (2200 feet)

Strong walkers could use these hills as part of a long weekend walk from Fairbourne on Barmouth Bay, crossing the whole of the Cader Idris ridge to Gau Craig, then by the Dovey Hills to Dinas Mawddwy, and on from there through Cwm Cywarch to the main Aran ridge, finally descending 45 kilometres (28 miles) later to Llanuwchllyn at the southern end of Bala Lake.

Route 8.8 The Tarren Hills from Abergynolwyn To speak of the Tarren *Hills* is tautology as 'Tarren' means 'hill'. But the phrase has stuck and made a convenient label for quite a few hills, though only two are over 600 metres. These grassy Tarren Hills, then, are of the kind that breeds in me a sense of utter contentment, made all the more acute by my inability to master the words best suited to describe the sensations I experience in their midst. Few hill areas in Wales possess this esoteric, almost fragile quality, the search for which has had me wandering the hills for years. This is something the Tarren Hills, in my opinion, share only with the Elan valley, the remote Carneddau, Mynydd Du and Fforest Fawr.

8.8a Tarrenhendre To reach Tarrenhendre from the north, start at the old quarrymen's village of Abergynolwyn in which there is a fine slate museum. Ascend steeply south out of the village by the metalled track leading to the Bryneglwys Quarries, among the remains of which there are some fine waterfalls. The way to the quarries is pleasant, easy walking, and the hillside on the right, across the Nant Gwernol, wooded and frequented by buzzards, while ahead Tarrenhendre forms the end of the cwm. There is a local tradition that this route through Nant Gwernol is a pilgrims' way to the holy island of Bardsey.

At Bryneglwys cross the stream and aim for the col between Tarrenhendre and the unnamed minor top to the east. The going here is more difficult, widespread re-afforestation having obscured the line of the paths shown on the map. But a route does remain, marked by occasion-

Sheltered Llyn Cyri, from which Craig y Llyn, left, takes its name. These grassy summits at the western end of the Cader Idris ridge are seldom visited, and provide excellent walking.

al wooden posts, and this soon leads to the col from where there is a breathtaking view of the Dovey estuary. From the col it is an easy ascent along a fence-line to the top of Tarrenhendre. Here two fences meet, and nearby there is a large cairn which you may mistake for the summit; it is not. The actual summit lies about 200 metres north, and is marked by another cairn adorned by a wooden post.

DISTANCE: 5 kilometres (3.1 miles)
ASCENT: 600 metres (1968 feet)

Tarrenhendre may, by this route, be conveniently linked with higher Tarren y Gesail to the north-east, though the actual line between the two will depend on how the new forest develops over the years. For the moment it is possible to keep to the crest of the connecting ridge, over

Tal y Llyn, south of Cader Idris.

the unnamed top and crossing Foel y Geifr, to gain the col, at a meeting of fences (716053 – where there is a stile), below a steepish pull to a large collapsed cairn. Here go left to reach the highest ground, the summit being marked by a trig point.

8.8b Tarren y Gesail Take the road to the Bryneglwys Quarries for about one kilometre (0.6 miles), until level ground is reached. Then ascend, left, on to a lower summit, Foel Pandy (not named on the 1:50 000 map, but indicated by its north-eastern face, Craig Wen). Continue up grassy slopes, south-east, to the summit.
DISTANCE: 4 kilometres (2.5 miles)
ASCENT: 630 metres (2065 feet)

A longer, easier ascent to Tarren y Gesail, probably better used as a descent, can be made by continuing to the quarries and from there finding a way through spoil heaps to a vague track leading into the eastern end of the cwm. This route joins the connecting ridge to Tarrenhendre at the meeting of fences (716053), and continues by the route described from there. En route you will cross Pont Llaeron, which is said to be of Roman origin; it is remarkably well preserved if it is. The dammed lake shown on the maps, presumably only used for the quarries, is no longer of any significance, and scarcely noticeable.

The ascent by this route is still 630 metres (2065 feet), though the distance increases to 6 kilometres (3.75 miles).

Route 8.9 Tarrenhendre from the Dovey valley Southwest from Tarrenhendre lies a vast area of open grassland, some of it now becoming afforested. Through the middle of it runs a superb grassy ridge terminating on the summit of Tarrenhendre; there is solitude and tranquillity in plenty here for those who seek it.

Start from 668997 on the minor road west of Pennal, and follow a rough track to 646001 where a minor path begins to ascend the hillside to the first of the summits, Trum Gelli. Continue along the ridge, rising all the time, over Tarren Cwm-ffernol and Mynydd Esgairweddan to the summit.

DISTANCE: 8.25 kilometres (5 miles)
ASCENT: 485 metres (1590 feet)

Routes of descent can easily be worked out from the summit of Tarrenhendre, but afforestation work has obscured many of the paths shown on the maps. On the other hand, it has introduced quite a number of new ones, and these can be used fairly easily to work out a way back to the vicinity of Pennal.

Section 9 – Arans

	MAP REFERENCE	HEIGHT (m)	1:50000 OS MAP
Aran Fawddwy	863224	905	124/125

Aran Benllyn	867243	885	124/125
Erw y Ddafad Ddu	865234	872	124/125
Glasgwm	837194	780	124/125
Foel Hafod Fynnyd	877227	689	124/125
Pen y Bryn Fforchog	818179	685	124/125
Gwaun y Llwyni	857205	685	124/125
Esgeiriau Gwynion	889236	671	124/125
Llechwedd Du	894224	614	124/125
Pen yr Allt Uchaf	869196	610	124/125
Y Gribin	843177	602	124/125

ROUTES
9.1 Aran Fawddwy from Cwm Cywarch
9.2 Aran Fawddwy from Rhydymain
9.3 Aran Benllyn from Llanuwchllyn

The Arans are a fine, compact group of hills south of Bala, that in recent years have seen a lot of aggravation over the question of access. The whole area is in many ownerships, and various landowners, some of them absentee, have objected to the presence of rock-climbers in particular on their land. In the early 1980s feelings led to a threatened mass trespass along the lines of Kinder Scout in the Peak District (and for that matter, Winter Hill, on the West Pennine Moors near Bolton.) It does seem that some climbers have caused problems. One local farmer told me that all basic courtesies were frequently disregarded as they tramped (and parked their cars) heedlessly on active farm land.

The upshot of all this trouble has been that walkers are now restricted to access, fortunately across the highest hills, by a Courtesy Path, the survival of which is subject to periodic review. The routes described here only use this Courtesy Path, and walkers wishing to visit other hills should seek permission first from the landowners. On the occasions that I have done so this permission has never been withheld, and I have always been thanked for taking the trouble to ask. So it is worth the effort, and please remember the advice on access on pages 13–14.

The peaks of Aran Fawddwy and Aran Benllyn from the shore of Llyn Tegid, Bala Lake.

The final stretch to the summit of Aran Fawddwy on the ascent from Cwm Cywarch.

There are three main areas of hills: the main ridge, a superb walk best done as a one-way traverse from Cywarch to Llanuwchllyn; the lonely, grassy hills on either side of Cwm Cywarch; and a small group of minor summits across the Llaethnant valley, easily accessible from Bwlch y Groes at the top of Cwm Cynllwyd, though they are often wet and boggy.

Route 9.1 Aran Fawddwy from Cwm Cywarch This ascent of Aran Fawddwy while undoubtedly popular is initially dull, principally because it passes through a deep trough, Hengwm, and so has restricted views until the watershed is reached. Even so, prominent at the head of Cwm Cywarch is the bold face of Craig Cwm Cywarch, and to its right the contrasting smooth profile of Gwaun y Llwyni.

From the lane through Cwm Cywarch a way-marked route starts across a bridge (853187) and leads north-east to an ascending traverse of the lower slopes of Pen yr Allt Uchaf (not named on the 1:50 000 map) to a quartz cairn at spot height 568. Beyond the cairn the path crosses boggy ground and climbs to the minor top, Dyrysgol, where the two Arans, Fawddwy and Benllyn, suddenly come into view. Beneath them lies Craiglyn Dyfi, the source of the river Dyfi. The path continues over level ground at first and then ascends to the neat top of Drws Bach where there is a small monument to a member of the RAF St Athan Mountain Rescue Team killed by lightning.

Continue from Drws Bach along the line of a fence to ascend the southern slopes of Aran Fawddwy where the going changes abruptly from grass to rock. The route is then indicated by a line of cairns, though the first large cairn to be encountered at the top of a rocky knoll is only the south summit, not the main summit as might be imagined. The highest point is still some distance away over more rocky terrain and is marked by a trig point.

DISTANCE: 6 kilometres (3.75 miles)
ASCENT: 760 metres (2495 feet)

Route 9.2 Aran Fawddwy from Rhydymain This line of
ascent is one of the recognised routes into the Arans, but it
has little to commend it. It starts off pleasantly enough,
running parallel with the Afon Harnog, but once above
the forest it becomes a struggle with open, trackless
moorland.

Begin by leaving the A494 Bala–Dolgellau trunk road a
short distance north of the village of Rhydymain at a minor
road (817229) signposted 'Gorsaf Drws y Nant Station'.
Follow this for just over half a kilometre to the bridge
spanning the Afon Harnog, Pont Gawr. This point may be
reached by car if you prefer, and with permission from the
farmer at nearby Esgair Gawr cars may be parked here.

Ascend the metalled road to Esgair Gawr, an old farmhouse with enormous, stone chimney pots, and at the
entrance to the farmyard go right along a Land Rover
track to a stile. The track ascends across a field to another
stile, and then follows a stone wall to a ruined building.
The retrospective view from here of Rhobell Fawr and
Dduallt is particularly impressive, with the bulk of both
mountains rising above the intervening landscape.

Continue from the ruined building to more stiles and on
to a vague path passing through a fire break in the forest.
The route is now delineated by the forest, and when a
forest road appears continue across it and over stiles,
passing through yet more forest finally to gain a much
wider break with the Afon Harnog below on the right.
There is a path through this break, but it is sketchy and
occasionally disappears into wet ground. The objective,
however, is the skyline ahead, and this marks the start of
open moorland.

Across the moorland the way is indicated by white
arrows painted on rocks and an occasional painted fence
post, but any path is more in the imagination than on the
ground. In mist this is a desolate area, and it seems to take
an interminable time before the rocky watershed of the
main Aran ridge is reached, running with which there is a
line of fence posts leading close to Aran Fawddwy's south

summit. The main summit, marked by a trig point, lies a short distance further north and provides a dramatic view down steep cliffs to Craiglyn Dyfi.

DISTANCE: (From the A494) 5.5 kilometres (3.4 miles)
ASCENT: 755 metres (2480 feet)

From Fawddwy a path descends northwards to a stile, and continues over the intermediate summit, Erw y Ddafad Ddu – *Black Sheep Acre* – to Aran Benllyn.

DISTANCE: 2 kilometres (1.25 miles)
ASCENT: 60 metres (200 feet)

Route 9.3 Aran Benllyn from Llanuwchllyn The long north ridge of Aran Benllyn provides an excellent introduction to the rugged, bumpy terrain that characterises much of the high ground of the Aran mountains. Off the main ridge, and indeed for much of the north ridge, the ground is grass and bog through which ancient upheavals have thrust high, craggy hills that provide excellent sport and far-reaching views.

Easy, grassy walking typifies the lower part of the ascent to Aran Fawddwy from Cwm Cywarch. Here the walkers are approaching the summit of Drws Bach.

Start at Pont y Pandy (880297), south-east of the village of Llanuwchllyn, where there is a small lay-by and a stile. A road runs parallel with the Afon Twrch for a short distance and climbs to a stile at a bridleway sign. Cross the field to another stile and continue around the small hill, Garth Fach, on a path alongside a fence. A long succession of stiles, always in line ahead, then leads towards Benllyn with the bulk of the mountain towering over the ridge. The view back northwards improves with height and reveals a wide panorama from Arenig Fawr and Moel Llyfnant to the Rhinogs, with the Snowdon massif looming in the centre distance.

Eventually the path starts to gain height significantly, passing the minor top, Moel Ffenigl, and climbs abruptly to a plateau containing a small lake, Llyn Pen Aran. The summit of Benllyn, marked by a large cairn, lies a few hundred metres further south, and requires a little more ascent.

The continuation southwards to Aran Fawddwy presents little difficulty, and passes first over the intermediate summit, Erw y Ddafad Ddu.

DISTANCE: 5.75 kilometres (3.6 miles)
ASCENT: 700 metres (2300 feet)

Section 10 – Berwyn Hills

	MAP REFERENCE	HEIGHT (m)	1:50 000 OS MAP
Moel Sych	066318	827	125
Cadair Berwyn	072327	827	125
Cadair Bronwen	077346	785	125
Tomle	085335	742	125
Foel Wen	099334	691	125
Mynydd Tarw	113324	681	125
Godor	094308	679	125
Cyrniau Nod	988279	667	125
Post Gwyn	048294	655	125
Foel Cwm Sian Llwyd	996314	648	125

Pen y Boncyn Trefeilw	963283	646	125
Moel Fferna	116398	630	125
Stac Rhos	969279	630	125
Foel y Geifr	937275	626	125
Moel y Cerrig Duon	923242	625	125
Unnamed summit (Moel Fferna)	089369	621	125
Cefn Gwyntog	976266	615	125
Trum y Gwrgedd	941284	612	125
Foel Goch	943291	610	125
Glan Hafon	078274	608	125
Unnamed summit (Moel y Cerrig Duon)	918258	606	125

ROUTES
10.1 The main Berwyn ridge from the Dee valley
10.2 Moel Sych and Cadair Berwyn from Tan y Pistyll
10.3 Moel Sych from Milltir Cerrig
10.4 Moel Fferna

The Berwyns are an immense range of rolling, heather-clad moorland hills which, were it not for the heather, would be immensely popular. As it is, a considerable portion of them fall at best into the category of 'sheer purgatory', leaving only the main Berwyn ridge of any real interest for the walker.

In the south-west, two tiered hills above Cwm Cynllwyd gaze across to the grandeur of the Aran range, while between them and the main ridge lies Hirnant, a vast intractable area from which local farmers struggle to gain some living. The north part of Hirnant is given to forestry, while the south serves as a water-catchment area feeding Lake Vyrnwy. The watershed forms the boundary of the Snowdonia National Park, and a route can be forced

Pistyll Rhaeadr, the highest waterfall in Wales. ▶

The eastern escarpment of the main Berwyn ridge, looking towards the two ▶▶
summits of Cadair Berwyn.

across it, particularly now that a new track has been blazed over part of it from the top of Cwm Hirnant. But 'force' is the operative word, and the area, though spectacular when the heather is in bloom, holds little of real interest apart from grouse and the occasional buzzard.

Thomas Pennant wrote of "multitudes of red grouse and a few black" on these hills in the 1770s. The 'few' black grouse of Pennant's day are however increasing in the forest at the head of Cwm Pennant.

The main Berwyn range is a much better place to walk. There are many options, allowing an intimate insight into a very relaxing part of Wales.

Route 10.1 The main Berwyn ridge from the Dee valley The three highest mountains of the Berwyn range form a line almost north to south, with Cadair Bronwen, one of the many legendary sites of King Arthur's Table, at the northern end, and Moel Sych, the highest summit, at the southern. Between these two, Cadair Berwyn is the only summit in the whole range to possess anything like cliffs, being flanked on the eastern side by an attractive steepness that sweeps to the valleys below. These cliffs are far too eroded and friable to interest the rock-climber, but a walk along their very edge gives an ever changing scene and much satisfaction to anyone who ventures there.

To reach the ridge from the Dee valley start from Hendwr (043385), about 3 kilometres (1.9 miles) south of the village of Cynwyd on the B4401. Take the minor road alongside the telephone box with the Afon Llynor bubbling by your side, and climb steadily, always ahead, to reach open pasture at a large 'No Trespassing' sign at spot height 323 on the 1:50000 map. The sign relates to the pasture itself, since the road you are on is a by-way open to all traffic, and is frequently used by motor cyclists. Keep the sign on your left, and continue ahead through a succession of gates, finally to emerge on to the open hillside near a small wooded area.

Continue ahead yet again, past a jumble of large rocks

strangely out of place in an otherwise grassy area. A short way further on a line of fence-posts marks the way through a mini morass (especially so in wet weather!). Once across this boggy section a better path is reached. Follow this to a final gate, just south-west of the minor top, Moel Pearce (063356 – not named on the 1:50 000 map), and continue ahead up a gentle rise to a small cairn where the path forks. The path to the right is the by-way, leading to the col between Cadair Bronwen and Cadair Berwyn, and gives easy access to either summit. The path to the left follows a fence-line (crossed at the top by a stile) to the summit of Cadair Bronwen, the highest point of which is marked by a large cairn.

DISTANCE: (To Cadair Bronwen) 5.5 kilometres (3.4 miles)

ASCENT: 625 metres (2050 feet)

From Cadair Berwyn the path continues to its south summit, and then on to Moel Sych.

Route 10.2 Moel Sych and Cadair Berwyn from Tan y Pistyll Pistyll Rhaeadr in its unique enclosed setting is one of the best waterfalls in Wales, dropping a total height only a little less than 100 metres, though the main fall is not so high. Above the falls the river is the Disgynfa, while below them it becomes the Rhaeadr, a rushing stream that has been an administrative boundary since the twelfth century, the counties of Denbigh and Montgomery eventually giving way to Clwyd and Powys.

Immediately below the falls stands the farm of Tan y Pistyll, though it is now given over largely to providing refreshments (including the alcoholic variety!) for visitors to the falls and the hills round about. There is a small charge for the car park, alongside which there are toilets. From the quiet of deeply snowclad hills I came to Tan y Pistyll one cold March day to share with unsuspected hordes of walkers the pleasure of warm, home-baked scones and cake ladled with jam and cream: I shall go again.

The broad, grassy summit of the main Berwyn ridge, looking south to Cadair Berwyn.

Adjoining Tan y Pistyll a gate gives access to the falls and to a track which runs behind the toilet block and through a small group of trees. The path, which is way-marked, eventually leads up and around to the top of the falls, but walkers bound for Moel Sych should leave it, at a signpost, and keep instead along a wide track leading into Nant y Llyn. Cross the river to gain a conspicuous rising track heading into the valley, and follow this, crossing the river twice more (once at 076311, and then a short distance further on), to the vicinity of Llyn Lluncaws beneath the steep slopes of Moel Sych and Cadair Berwyn where the path becomes indistinct.

For Moel Sych make for the obvious col, south-west, between it and a lower, grassy bump, and ascend by a fence-line, with stiles where you need them.

For Cadair Berwyn ascend east to a stile overlooking Cwm Maen Gwynedd, and then climb very steeply along the fence-line to a point just south of Berwyn's south summit; the trig point lies about 400 metres to the north.

Cadair Bronwen, at the northern end of the main Berwyn ridge, is one of the legendary sites of King Arthur's Table.

Since both Moel Sych and Cadair Berwyn are of the same metric height (Moel Sych is actually one foot higher!) the amount of ascent from Tan y Pistyll is the same, as is the distance – Cadair Berwyn, though more distant, is on a more direct line.

DISTANCE: 3.5 kilometres (2.2 miles)
ASCENT: 520 metres (1705 feet)

Route 10.3 Moel Sych from Milltir Cerrig This highest summit of the Berwyn range is most easily ascended from the south-west by a narrow track which struggles through deep heather.

Start from Milltir Cerrig at the top of the B4391 which runs from the village of Llangynog to Bala. At the top of the pass, which is sometimes blocked in winter and marks the boundary between the former counties of Merioneth and Montgomery, a track descends (at 018303) to Llandrillo in the Dee valley. Follow this track for a short distance until it heads left, and leave it for a narrow path ascending north-east along a long grassy arm to Moel Sych. Anyone with an aversion to the insect life which inhabits heather during the summer months is advised to stay away from this route, the delights of which are better appreciated in spring and autumn.

DISTANCE: 5 kilometres (3.1 miles)
ASCENT: 350 metres (1150 feet)

Route 10.4 Moel Fferna The most northerly of the Berwyn Hills, Moel Fferna, lies 5 kilometres (3.1 miles) south-east of the market town of Corwen, and is an ideal walk for a short day. Much of Berwyn country is densely covered with heather, Moel Fferna being no exception, and it affords excellent cover for grouse.

The easiest approach is from Llidiart y Parc (119433) on the A5, east of Corwen. Directly opposite the point where the B5437 leaves the A5, two lanes head south. Take the right-hand lane until a stream is reached, and then follow a track on the left which leads to the by-way shown on the map. This is sometimes difficult to follow, but heads for a cleared and re-planted area of old forest, and from there to the forest boundary. Moel Fferna is now clearly in view ahead, and can be reached on a good path (passing just below the summit) and a Land Rover track ascending to the summit trig.

DISTANCE: 4 kilometres (2.5 miles)
ASCENT: 480 metres (1575 feet)

Section 11 – Plynlimon

	MAP REFERENCE	HEIGHT (m)	1:50000 OS MAP
Pen Pumlumon Fawr	789869	752	135
Pen Pumlumon Arwystli	815877	741	135
Unnamed summit (Pumlumonfawr)	799872	727	135
Y Garn	776852	684	135
Pumlumon Fach	789874	668	135
Unnamed summit (Pumlumon Fach)	787875	664	135
Pumlumon Cwmbiga	831899	620	135

ROUTE
11.1 Pen Pumlumon Fawr from Eisteddfa Gurig

Black's *Picturesque Guide to North Wales* describes Plinlimmon (sic) as "the most dangerous mountain in Wales", owing to the "frequency of bogs, concealed under a smooth and apparently firm turf". And goes on to express the view that "few travellers who make the ascent deem themselves recompensed for the toil and hazard". Here was a view shared by the Reverend W. Bingley, who wrote: "From the various accounts that had reached me respecting this mountain, there did not appear any probable compensation for my trouble in going so far out of my road to ascend its summit, I therefore continued my route, and only passed it at a distance." Less daunted however was George Borrow who, after breakfast at Dyffryn Castell, strode across the mountain in his journey through "Wild Wales".

Perhaps the timidity shown by early travellers had something to do with the fact that Plynlimon holds a significant place in Welsh history, as a scene of turmoil. Its morasses (such as they are) have witnessed many a struggle. An exterminating warfare was carried on here between Owain Cyfeilog, Prince of Powys, and Hywel ap Cadogan; here it was, too, that the ubiquitous Owain Glyndŵr unfurled the banner of Welsh independence, and hence in the summer of 1401 harassed the adjacent countryside, sacked Montgomery, burned Welshpool, and destroyed the Abbey of Cwm Hir.

But the greatest feature of Plynlimon must surely be that within its recesses three major rivers, the Rheidol, the Wye and the Severn, all have their source, flowing great distances to the sea and providing en route some of the most fertile and beautiful countryside in the whole of Wales.

Plynlimon, in its widest sense, consists of a vast group of mountains of which three in particular are pre-eminent. On these three are piles of stones, principally five in number, Pumlumon, *Five Stacks*, commonly alleged to cover the remains of warriors slain in battle, and serving as memorials to their exploits. For reasons that are obscure, and notwithstanding the common usage among the Welsh people of the name 'Pumlumon', the hill-walking fraternity seem to have anglicised the name to 'Plynlimon'. For the general area I have done the same, but have reverted to the Welsh, as is proper, for the mountain names. The Ordnance Survey hedges its bets the same way.

Route 11.1 Pen Pumlumon Fawr from Eisteddfa Gurig
There is no reason, in spite of all the warnings of early writers, not to visit Plynlimon. It is excellent walking country with many interesting ups and downs, though it does not lend itself readily to circular walks.

For the ascent of Pen Pumlumon Fawr, start at Eisteddfa Gurig (797841), where for a fee you may park your car, and take the farm track at the west of the farm buildings. The main gate is frequently locked, and you may have to ask at the farm for it to be opened, but the start of the route is along a 'Road used as a footpath' and so may legitimately be used. Proceed along this track, and after a short distance cross the stream flowing down from the old mines in the wide cwm beneath Pen Pumlumon Fawr. Follow the path, which becomes boggy as it nears the mines, and then, in the vicinity of the mines, turn left to follow a line of wooden posts (sometimes missing) over rising ground to the summit cairn.

DISTANCE: 3.5 kilometres (2.2 miles)
ASCENT: 430 metres (1410 feet)

The view from the summit is particularly impressive, and an easy extension may be made along a fence-line to the unnamed summit to the east of Pen Pumlumon Fawr, on either side of which rise the Rheidol and the Wye.

From the unnamed summit, Pencerrigtewion lies a short way north, with Pen Pumlumon Arwystli not much further east. Alternatively an easy descent south will return you to the old mines encountered on the ascent.

Section 12 – Radnor Forest

	MAP REFERENCE	HEIGHT (m)	1:50 000 OS MAP
Great Rhos	182639	660	148
Black Mixen	196644	650	148
Unnamed summit (Black Mixen)	198636	640c	148
Bache Hill	214636	610	137/148

ROUTES
12.1 Bache Hill and Black Mixen from New Radnor
12.2 Great Rhos

Walks into Radnor Forest centre on the village of New Radnor where car parking may be found near the Cornewall-Lewis Memorial Cross in Water Street, or at the start of the lane, Mutton Dingle. The village was once important enough to have given its name to the county (which was created in 1536 during the reign of Henry VIII out of the unshired lands of the Borders, or Marches, and abolished in 1974 when it became part of Powys under local-government re-organisation). But Presteigne, on the border with England, has long since been the centre for county activities, leaving Radnor to dwindle to its present picturesque-village status.

Although the former county of Radnor is of comparatively modern derivation, the name, Radnor, as it applies to the Forest and to Old and New Radnor, is a very old one. Even *New* Radnor is at least as old as the Domesday Book (1086–7).

A hundred years after the Domesday Book Archbishop Baldwin of Canterbury began his mission to preach the Crusades in Wales at New Radnor, and it was here that Gerald of Wales records he himself was the first to stand up and take the sign of the Cross. Gerald's own career as a crusader didn't take him beyond France, while the Archbishop, who kept his vow, perished for his pains at the siege of Acre. Together on their fund-raising journey they visited Cruker Castle which was to be destroyed in 1401 by Owain Glyndŵr "who at the same time beheaded the garrison of sixty men in the castle yard". For two and a half centuries, from the time of the Normans, much of this part of Wales was unhappy territory, where legalised oppressors, the Lords Marchers, held power of life and death over the inhabitants, ruling them by the sword under the *Jura Regalia* – a most severe form of martial law.

The Forest, too, a place in spite of its name of bare open hills affording pasturage to horses and sheep, was once a bounded forest, that is an area into which "if any man or beast entered . . . without leave, the former was to lose a limb and the latter to be forfeited, unless a heavy ransom were paid and other grievous exactions submitted to". Fortunately for the modern walker this was remedied in the reign of Elizabeth I, yet, with the presence in the deep V-shaped valley at the centre of this tract of countryside of an active ammunition-testing range, there is still no guarantee of safety to life and limb.

Route 12.1 Bache Hill and Black Mixen from New Radnor The ascent of Bache Hill and Black Mixen is an enjoyable experience made more so by its unexpectedness, if you, as I used to, tend to think that Welsh mountains begin and end with Snowdonia and the Brecon Beacons. I have now come to regard this area of rolling hills as something of a gem.

To ascend Bache Hill, start up the lane, Mutton Dingle, in the centre of the village and climb quite steeply on a metalled roadway to a point where the road forks, going right, into forestry plantations, and left along a short track to a gate. Beyond the gate the track continues, rising gently and giving superb distant views as far as the conspicuous flat tops of the Brecon Beacons. As the track rises it opens up a view, too, into and across the deep trough of Harley Dingle, with the Three Riggles on Great Rhos quite prominent. Eventually the track reaches the top of the forest which has thus far accompanied us, and arrives at a gate giving access to the towering mound of Whimble, a minor summit well worth a diversion for the views it affords of the Border Hills.

From the gate continue on an obvious path above the narrow defile containing Ystol Bach Brook to what can only be described as an alp in the true sense of a high mountain pasture. This meadow, which when I last visited it was boasting a healthy crop of turnips, took ten years to establish, and lies on a col formed by meltwaters escaping from a glacial lake in Harley Dingle. Above the meadow rise Whinyard Rocks, though they are unstable and of no interest to the climber, and beneath them one autumn I noted a line of bee-hives, with companions to be found higher up amid the heather of Bache Hill and on Black Mixen.

It is possible to walk beneath Whinyard Rocks and then to ascend by one of a number of narrow paths on to the higher ground leading across to Bache Hill. Alas, the heather really justifies changing the spelling of Bache to B-a-s-h. Fortunately, there is an easier alternative going left from the gate which gave access to Whinyard Rocks, and this climbs gently until the summit of Bache Hill appears on the right. Once on easier intermediate ground a diversion, right, will enable you to reach the summit, though not without tackling some deep heather in the final few metres. The view from the summit trig point is tremendous, and no description I could give of it would do it justice. I have been fortunate in never having been there when the bilberries were ripe, otherwise I might still be there, munching quietly!

DISTANCE: 4.5 kilometres (2.8 miles)
ASCENT: 375 metres (1230 feet)

The continuation to Black Mixen requires a return to an obvious col (206638), rising on the left of which is a path that leads on to the unnamed summit (198636) above the steep escarpment known as Great Creigiau. Pass instead through a gate and over a stile to gain a graded forestry track which climbs gently and, as the aerial on Black Mixen comes into view, forks. Keep left to a gate, beyond which the track continues to the Transmitter Station, and the nearby summit trig point.

DISTANCE: 2 kilometres (1.25 miles)
ASCENT: 70 metres (230 feet)

From the summit it is easier to return the way you have come, but there are paths through the abundant heather, and strong walkers will enjoy a return over the unnamed summit back to the col. At Whinyard Rocks a left turn will lead to a gate at the end of the meadow, giving access to the upper part of the forestry land and to forest trails leading to a small summit, Knowle Hill (214617), and back along a track to Mutton Dingle.

To continue to Great Rhos, which is strongly recommended, return from the trig point to the aerial and head west to a prominent wooden post, picking up a sketchy path leading around the rim of Harley Dingle to the edge of more forest. Cross the col at the head of Harley Dingle and stay with the forest edge, an area where I have identified the presence of foxes, to meet a fence. Beyond the fence turn right, staying with the boundary of the forest to meet a Land Rover track emerging from the forest. Keep left along this; it shortly runs parallel with another fence and then forks, the main track leaving the fence and heading for the summit trig point which has now come into view. The track does not, however, cross the summit, passing a short way north of it, and disappears altogether a short while after. In misty conditions good compass work is essential here, though anyone in difficulty could, with care, find a way down into Harley Dingle, but walkers are reminded that the upper part of this valley is used for ammunition testing.

DISTANCE: 2.5 kilometres (1.6 miles)
ASCENT: 55 metres (180 feet)

Route 12.2 describes a walk to Great Rhos, and the descent of this, leading back to New Radnor, will provide a pleasant end to a fine circular walk of about 14 kilometres (8.75 miles).

Route 12.2 Great Rhos Probably the star attraction of Radnor Forest is a magnificent triple cascade of water, imaginatively named Water-break-its-neck. It lies just above forestry plantations to the west of Fron Hill (194609), about 3 kilometres (1.9 miles) west of New Radnor. Thomas Roscoe, who travelled through Wales in the early part of the nineteenth century comments: "The rocks form a narrow, high amphitheatre, over which the water is precipitated in scattered portions, and, falling into a dark pool, meanders away among the fragments of rock until it gains the more open glen."

The Three Riggles on Great Rhos.

Whinyard Rocks, Bache Hill.

The upper section of Harley Dingle.

To reach the falls, and so to start the ascent of Great Rhos (which seems at some time in the past to have been known as Glastwyn), take the track, north, leaving the A44 at 194593. This leads into, and climbs through, the Warren Plantations and, on leaving the forest, provides, on the left, a fine vantage point for viewing the falls. There is a path around the falls crossing a tiny bridge above the upper falls and heading back into the plantations. A rising track then leads through the forest to a stile (183619) from where it is a short walk, crossing a ford (not marked on the 1:50000 map) into a long gully known as Davy Morgan's Dingle (likewise not marked). The bed of the gully should be followed upstream until, at the top of it, a traverse over more level ground, some of it damaged by fire in 1976, will lead to a fence and then on, through heather, to the trig point on the summit of Great Rhos.

DISTANCE: 5.25 kilometres (3.3 miles)
ASCENT: 400 metres (1310 feet)

Return across the area of burnt peat, using tracks bull-dozed to combat the fire, and head for the col between Great Rhos and Fron Hill where it is possible to gain an old slate quarry the upper part of which has been left with some interesting rock formations. A bridleway meets the col from the direction of Davy Morgan's Dingle, passing through a gate and on to a pleasant descending track across the east flank of Fron Hill.

In the valley bottom cross the river, Harley Brook, by a precarious plank bridge to join a metalled road. This leads back to the A44, joining it at Haine's Mill.

Walkers who are heading back to New Radnor will find a more interesting return along a track, left, just after reaching the metalled road. This leads through two gates and eventually to New Radnor at Newgate Lane, only a few minutes from the starting point of Route 12.1.

Section 13 – Elan and Ystwyth Valleys

	MAP REFERENCE	HEIGHT (m)	1:50 000 OS MAP
Elan valley			
Drygarn Fawr	862584	641	147
Gorllwyn	918591	613	147
Y Gamriw	944612	604	147
Drum yr Eira	851589	600c	147
Ystwyth valley			
Pen y Garn (Bryn Garw)	798771	610	135

ROUTES
13.1 Drygarn Fawr from the Irfon valley
13.2 Drygarn Fawr and Gorllwyn from Caban Coch reservoir
13.3 Pen y Garn from Cwmystwyth

Due west of the quiet little town of Rhayader lies a remarkable range of hills that is at once captivating and enigmatic. They are the Cwmdeuddwr Hills, now serving mainly to feed the vast reservoirs constructed by the damming of the Elan and Claerwen rivers. (The name 'Cwmdeuddwr' means 'The valley of the Two Waters'.) At the northern end of the range the infant Afon Elan and the Ystwyth are born, travelling for a few kilometres in parallel but opposite directions before the former turns south-east to meander through wide, open grassland. Between them runs the old mountain road (now an easy, pleasant drive) from Devil's Bridge to Rhayader. Part of its length, from Devil's Bridge to Blaenycwm (826756) is an old drove road, and nearby Tyllwyd was once a drovers' inn. From Blaenycwm the drovers would head north-east to reach what is now the A44 near Llangurig, or they could make across the hills further down the valley from Bodtalog. Either way had its problems, since it was fairly common knowledge that many drovers who were going this way had contracted with gold miners to carry their bullion to London. The short cut across the mountains was as a result often a hazardous business. The valley was also an ill-fated place in other ways, for it was here that the Rebecca Riots took place. These took the form of systematic attacks on the toll gates put up by landowners to fund road-improvement schemes, though many records tell of cattle sinking belly deep along some stretches of the road. Now, with the damming of a good part of the valley, they would have to swim their way to market.

From the valleys the hills promise much for the walker, yet on the tops that promise never seems to be fulfilled. Or does it? . . . Every time I walk these barren hills I come away with a feeling that there is much more about them than I have been permitted to see. The hills themselves are windswept, empty grassland, unfit for sheep and offering little sustenance for all but the hardiest birds. The absence of fences, walls, and buildings of any kind testifies that there is little here for man – though the Forestry Commission are now directing their attention to the northern and southern ends of the range. The whole area is bewildering, and fatal for anyone caught in mist. Yet it puzzles me that I cannot identify the strong attraction I experience.

I would not put these hills high on my list of places to visit again and again (though I have done so!), but I would certainly not omit them!

Route 13.1 Drygarn Fawr from the Irfon valley The Afon Irfon rising to the north-west of Drygarn Fawr flows eventually to join the Wye at Builth Wells, offering throughout its whole length the most picturesque scenery, but nowhere more so than near its source north of the village of Abergwesyn. The valley here narrows and twists in and out of craggy hillsides in a way that reminds one of the Scottish highlands, coming finally to a wider section at Llannerch-yrfa (836556). The ascent of Drygarn Fawr from here is simple and impressive, though recent forestry work has drastically changed the face of the map.

Start along the graded track, before the road crosses the river, and ascend gradually through fairly new forest. Stay on the graded track as it twists around, first left and then right, before arriving at the top of the forest and a gate. Do not attempt to follow the bridleway shown on the map.

At the gate turn left and leave the graded track. Continue in a north-easterly direction on a vague path, occasionally marked by yellow posts (some of which are misleading!), and descend to cross the Afon Gwesyn near its source. Drygarn Fawr, with its immaculately constructed bee-hive cairns, lies directly ahead across rough, rising ground.

DISTANCE: 5 kilometres (3.1 miles)
ASCENT: 300 metres (985 feet)

Route 13.2 Drygarn Fawr and Gorllwyn from Caban Coch reservoir The ascent of Drygarn Fawr both from the north and from the south starts through pleasant valleys, but each gives way eventually to the bleakness that is typical of the Cwmdeuddwr Hills. The ascent from the north, not as attractive in my view as that from Llannerch-yrfa, nevertheless offers a fine tourist approach along the Caban Coch reservoir.

In the exceptional drought of 1984 the drowned village of Nant Gwyllt, normally under seventy feet of water, reappeared near the foot of this reservoir, and the garden walls of Nantgwyllt House where Shelley wrote *Queen Mab* were clearly visible. Shelley had at one time thought of buying this property. Maybe if he had, Birmingham might have had to look elsewhere for its water supply a century later.

Start the walk from a small parking space near the telephone box at 901616, and descend to cross the bridge over what remains of the Afon Claerwen. It was here, in the small copse near the bridge, that I once observed in the space of only ten minutes a pair of Willow Tits, a Pied Flycatcher, four Great Tits, and two very food-orientated Nuthatches studiously ignoring my presence in their search for insects. Across the bridge, head for the nearby farm, Llannerch-y-cawr, but just as the road forks, double back, right, along the road leading to Rhiwnant. Again after only a short distance leave this road for a Land Rover track on the left, and pass through a gate. Continue along this good track, with fine views into Cwm Rhiwnant opening up on the right, and ascend into Cwm Paradwys. When the track doubles back, left, to make easier work of the hillside, keep ahead on a narrow track running with the Nant Paradwys, and follow this, indistinct in places, all the way to the watershed at Bwlch-y-ddau-faen. There is a temptation, most definitely to be resisted, to ascend to a stone shelter, marked as a cairn on the map (897598), and to try to reach Gorllwyn from there. The effort expended struggling with the terrain would be out of all proportion to such doubtful saving in distance as there may seem.

From the watershed Drygarn Fawr lies 3.5 kilometres (2.2 miles) west; Gorllwyn, 2.5 kilometres (1.6 miles) east. Both involve tackling rough, grassy moorland with few identifying features, making this a hazardous undertaking in misty conditions, but an exceptionally rewarding one

Ascending into Nant Paradwys, south-west of the Elan valley.

on a fine summer's day (providing you are carrying sufficient liquid!).

DISTANCE: Drygarn Fawr 7.5 kilometres (4.7 miles)
             Gorllwyn 6.5 kilometres (4.1 miles)
ASCENT: Drygarn Fawr 370 metres (1215 feet)
           Gorllwyn 340 metres (1115 feet)

Route 13.3 Pen y Garn from Cwmystwyth The route to Pen y Garn (also known as Bryn Garw) starts north of Cwmystwyth at 792754 through a gate and along a former farm track which leads to a small group of ruined buildings. Continue past the ruins to another gate, and immediately after the gate ascend steeply, right, to gain a new forest track leading, right again, to a new iron gate.

From the iron gate ascend over grass to a cluster of shooting butts, and then move right to gain the long ridge of Penlan Fawr extending south from distant Pen y Garn.

The dam of Pen-y-garreg reservoir.   ▶

The top of this long ridge is crossed by Land Rover tracks, and these lead to a fence-line where wide forest tracks begin – though as yet there are no trees. The track passes just below the summit of Pen y Garn, which is adorned by a circular stone shelter, a trig point, and a fenced area of experimental grassland.

DISTANCE: 2 kilometres (1.25 miles)
ASCENT: 220 metres (720 feet)

This is an attractive, simple walk, with wide ranging views in all directions. It can be made even simpler, but becomes boring, by following uninteresting graded tracks from 784753.

Section 14 – Black Mountains

	MAP REFERENCE	HEIGHT (m)	1:50000 OS MAP
Waun Fach	215300	810	161
Pen y Gadair Fawr	229287	800	161
Pen Allt Mawr	207243	719	161
Pen Rhos Dirion	212334	713	161
Pen Cerrig Calch	217223	701	161
Twmpa	225350	690	161
Chwarel y Fan	258294	679	161
Hay Bluff (Pen y Beacon)	244366	677	161
Mynydd Llysiau	207279	663	161
Pen Twyn Mawr	242267	658	161
Pen Twyn Glas	213257	646	161
Mynydd Troed	166293	609	161
Mynydd Pen-y-fal (Sugar Loaf)	273187	596	161
Crug Hywel (Table Mountain)	225207	451	161

Appendix
In addition to the above summits there are a further four hills in the group known as the Black Mountains, three of them with their highest points almost exactly on the border with England.

The distant Black Mountains.

The fourth, Black Hill, is wholly in England. They are added here for completeness.

Black Mountain	255350	703	161
Black Hill	275348	640	161
Black Daren	267322	637	161
North Daren	277311	616	161

ROUTES

The Black Mountains, on the border between Wales and England, are a paradise for the walker who revels in long and lofty ridges separated by valleys of quiet calm. Once they were an area of complete and uncompromising solitude, now they resound to the tread of walkers and pony trekkers alike. Yet still with their beauty they amaze the visitor of today just as much as they did Bishop Roger of Salisbury who, speaking of Llanthony Priory, opined to Henry I that "it had cloisters for the building of which the whole treasure of the realm would not suffice". He was, of course, speaking of the immense girdle of mountains.

The whole area roughly resembles a hand laid flat. The fingers are the ridges Allt Mawr in the west, Waun Fach, Ffwddog, Hatterall (the boundary with England), and the Cat's Back – the Black Hill ridge. The intervening spaces are the valleys, west to east, of Grwyne Fechan, Grwyne Fawr, the Vale of Ewyas and the Olchon. To top the whole thing off, or more accurately to round it off, the dome of Pen-y-fal (Sugar Loaf as it is more popularly known), recognisable from afar, is a marvellous and easy short walk by any standards.

Although part of the Black Mountains are in England, and this book is primarily concerned with the 600-metre mountains of Wales, these pedantic criteria have been suspended in dealing with this part of the country so as to present a complete picture, and for the simple reason that it would seem puerile of me to ostracise otherwise worthy hills just because some ancient geological upheaval didn't match up to present-day demarcations!

Route 14.1 Hay Bluff and Black Mountain Hay Bluff, known also as Pen y Beacon, and the higher summit to the south at 703 metres (known locally as Black Mountain), lie on or near the Offa's Dyke Path. They are both easily reached from the stone circle – only half a circle in reality – at 239374, where there is a car park. Across the road from the stone circle a path ascends very steeply up the escarpment of Hay Bluff to the trig point on the summit. It is an ascent calling for strong calf muscles, but respite appears in the form of a rising path, diverting to the right half-way up the ascent. From the top of the direct ascent turn right to reach the summit; from the end of the path go left.

DISTANCE: 1 kilometre (0.6 miles)
ASCENT: 200 metres (655 feet)

The continuation to Black Mountain is by a well-worn path, boggy in places, which joins the Offa's Dyke Path after a little more than one kilometre (0.6 miles), and then climbs easily to the summit (unnamed on maps). The Offa's Dyke Path carries on from Black Mountain in a south-easterly direction along the Hatterall Ridge, crossing the summits of Black Daren, North Daren and finally the minor top, Red Daren, though the 1:50000 map misleads about the location of Black Daren.

From the top of Hay Bluff a peaty track along the west escarpment descends to meet the Llanthony–Capel-y-ffin

The summit trig on Hay Bluff.

road at the Gospel Pass (Bwlch yr Efengyl). The pass may take its name, like many features in this area, from the preaching and crusade fund-raising activities of the Archdeacon of Brecon, Gerald of Wales, and Archbishop Baldwin of Canterbury, in the late twelfth century.

Route 14.2 Twmpa This neat little summit is easily climbed by a well-worn path ascending from the Gospel Pass (236351) at the head of the Llanthony–Capel-y-ffin road. The top, marked by a small cairn, is reached without difficulty, and provides a panoramic view north-west across the Wye valley, with its numerous caravans of pony trekkers, to the Begwns and on towards Radnor Forest.
DISTANCE: 1 kilometre (0.6 miles)
ASCENT: 150 metres (490 feet)

The continuation south to Pen Rhos Dirion follows a path roughly parallel with the escarpment to the summit trig point. It is nowhere difficult, and the rising air currents created by the escarpment are much favoured by glider pilots.

Route 14.3 Chwarel y Fan and Pen Rhos Dirion This route is typical of many in South Wales, and in the Black Mountains in particular, involving a short, sharp start followed by long and gently undulating, grassy ridges with a tremendous sense of openness. The going underfoot is generally easy, and, when the conditions are right, it is ideal terrain for cross-country ski-ing and winter walking.

The Mynydd Du Forest, where this route starts, offers pleasant walking in itself, and is well provided with car parks and picnic areas to serve as starting points. The most convenient of these is at the end of the metalled roadway,

Twmpa is easily reached by a short walk from the top of the Gospel Pass. ▲

Semi-wild ponies feed peacefully on the summit of Pen Rhos Dirion. ▶

near Blaen y Cwm, at 253286, where the track forks. The lower road leads to the Grwyne Fawr reservoir some 3 kilometres (1.9 miles) distant following the course of the bubbling river (occasionally a torrent) issuing from the reservoir. The higher road climbs along the edge of the forest, and eventually leads through the length of the Grwyne Fawr valley to the escarpment overlooking the Wye valley to the north. This ambling walk through the valley, while presenting no spectacular views, is nevertheless a pleasant jaunt for anyone wanting a simple walk without too much effort. The trip to the escarpment and back is about 12 kilometres (7.5 miles).

For Chwarel y Fan take the higher road, below the forest, and on reaching the northern edge of the forest turn right and ascend along the fence-line on a vague track until the broad summit of the ridge is gained. Chwarel y Fan then lies a short distance south-east, its summit being marked by a large cairn near to which the remains of old quarry workings (*chwarel* in Welsh) provide shelter if needed.

DISTANCE: 1.75 kilometres (1.1 miles)

ASCENT: 280 metres (920 feet)

The continuation to Pen Rhos Dirion is in a north-westerly direction, along a broad, grassy and heathery ridge, and passes first over the minor top, Twyn Tal y Cefn, with its highest point marked by a small cairn the stones of which on my last visit (in 1983) were painted red, white and blue, though in commemoration of what is not certain.

The summit of Pen Rhos Dirion is adorned by a trig point set back a few metres from the edge of the escarpment. Here I once spent a very contented hour dangling my feet over the edge of the escarpment, blissfully contemplating the breathtaking scenery, much at peace with my companion, and both of us absorbed by the hovering kestrels and soaring buzzards vying for air space with gliders. Far below us, as if in another world, trains of pony

trekkers meandered along a network of bridleways, as a large herd of wild ponies crept up on us from behind, placidly munching their way across the hills.
DISTANCE: 6 kilometres (3.75 miles)
ASCENT: 100 metres (330 feet)

A return down the Grwyne Fawr valley for those who feel able to leave such a delectable spot requires only a kilometre's walk south-west to join the track leading south-east into the valley. A better alternative is to continue over the minor top, Pen y Manllwyn, to Waun Fach and Pen y Gadair Fawr (see Route 14.4), and to return to the start from there.

Route 14.4 Waun Fach and Pen y Gadair Fawr Route 14.3 describes the pleasant walk through the Grwyne Fawr valley to the north-west escarpment overlooking the Wye valley, and walkers who prefer not to tackle steep ascents early in the day will find the valley a gentle awakening, though I must confess to having almost fallen asleep beside the reservoir one fine summer's day.

On reaching the escarpment turn left to pick up a track which crosses the minor top, Pen y Manllwyn, and then skirts the rim of the beautiful Rhiangoll valley beyond which the lump of Mynydd Troed rises above a patchwork of farm fields. There follows a short ascent to the peaty summit plateau of Waun Fach, at 810 metres the highest of the Black Mountains, which is marked by a small cairn.
DISTANCE: 9 kilometres (5.6 miles)
ASCENT: 410 metres (1345 feet)

The ridge of Pen Trumau descends west from Waun Fach, connecting the higher ridge with the one leading from Mynydd Llysiau to Pen Cerrig Calch. This makes an excellent, long rambling walk for those who do not have to return to first base.

The continuation, however, from Waun Fach south-east to Pen y Gadair Fawr is in part trackless and often

The summit of Pen y Gadair Fawr can only be reached from the north by negotiating an unpleasant boggy section of ground.

boggy. A compass bearing or two would be advisable in misty conditions.

DISTANCE: 2 kilometres (1.25 miles)
ASCENT: 65 metres (215 feet)

From the summit of Pen y Gadair Fawr, which is marked by a large pile of stones, a return (2 kilometres, 1.25 miles) may be made to the start in the Grwyne Fawr valley by heading south-east to meet the edge of the Mynydd Du Forest and then descending very steeply along the forest boundary until it reaches the river Grwyne. The river can usually be crossed without too much difficulty, though it can be a problem when in spate. In view of this it is wise to determine before setting off up the valley whether, on the return descent, you feel you could get across, otherwise a long detour to the reservoir could be in the offing. Some of

The summit of Pen y Gadair Fawr. The hills in the background are Pen Allt Mawr and Pen Cerrig Calch.

the steepness of the descent along the forest boundary, which basically follows the line of a broad gully, can be avoided by staying on the north side of the gully and keeping to the open hillside.

Route 14.5 Waun Fach from the Rhiangoll valley The peaty summit of the highest of the Black Mountains, Waun Fach, may be reached quite easily from the Rhiangoll valley by two routes. Both are a pleasure to walk, and choosing between them is difficult. The logical solution, of course, is to combine the two in a shortish excursion, something not to be discounted as a worthwhile introduction to these hills. The first route (14.5a) starts at Pengenffordd (173301), the second (14.5b) at 186289.

14.5a This ascent starts at the highest point of the Crickhowell to Talgarth road (A479), near a telephone box. It is just possible to park here, but it is more advisable to ask permission at the Castle Inn (174296) to use the hotel car park; in any case the circular walk taking in both routes described here makes it immaterial where you start or finish (providing it's at the same place!).

Follow the lane on the right of the telephone box through trees to a metalled road. Turn left and at the end of the road take to a signposted public footpath, and follow a deeply furrowed track to the start of the long descending ridge, Y Grib, at the foot of which are the remains of a late twelfth-century fortification, Castell Dinas. Once on the ridge take a line up the centre, steeply at first, but then, as it undulates over a series of bumps, easing to a pleasant gradual ascent. This ridge, which affords a good view of the Rhiangoll valley, ascends not to Waun Fach, but to the minor top, Pen y Manllwyn. There are many paths across the ridge, particularly at Bwlch Bach-ar-grib (just after the second bump), but the route up the centre presents little difficulty. Leave it as you approach the head of Cwm y Nant, on the left, and follow a less distinct path right to Pen y Manllwyn.

The continuation, south-east and then south to Waun Fach, while boggy, should present few problems, except perhaps in mist when a compass bearing may help.

DISTANCE: 5.5 kilometres (3.4 miles)
ASCENT: 490 metres (1605 feet)

14.5b This ascent also provides a way on to the Allt Mawr ridge (Route 14.7), and has the attraction of a fairly gradual start accompanied by beautiful views.

Start from the road junction at 186289 where a car or two can be tidily left, and ascend east through a tunnel of trees to a series of gates forming part of sheep enclosures. A path then ascends the broad shoulder of the minor top, Pen Trumau, to the col between it and Mynydd Llysiau. Thereafter the walk around the head of the Grwyne

Fechan, across Pen Trumau, to Waun Fach presents no problems.
DISTANCE: 4 kilometres (2.5 miles)
ASCENT: 520 metres (1705 feet)

The connecting bit of roadway between the respective starting points can be avoided for a lot of the way since a diversion past the Cwm Fforest Riding Centre allows a minor track to be taken to or from the Castle Inn.

Route 14.6 Pen y Gadair Fawr from Llanbedr This ascent, which can easily be extended to include Waun Fach, involves a long walk across an ascending grassy ridge with forest on the right and the beautiful Grwyne Fechan valley on the left. Strong walkers can make a most rewarding round tour by continuing to the Mynydd Llysiau–Pen Cerrig Calch ridge and descending, at the end of a fairly long day, to Crug Hywel (Table Mountain).

Start from the road junction at 234203 (where it is possible to park one or two cars), a short distance west of Llanbedr village, and take the lane down to the village. Continue along the lane past the church, which soon deteriorates into a track and descends to the river. Cross the bridge, but ignore the obvious track alongside the river and keep ahead instead along a less obvious track climbing steeply upwards. Half-way up the hillside go left to a stile, and then continue to a stone stile at the roadway. Cross the road and head for another stone stile in the top right-hand corner of the field, then keep to the left of the farm, Hen-bant, and continue to a gate and a stile and, after the farm, another gate. At this gate turn left to yet another gate leading on to an enclosed track which eventually (thankfully!) leads to open country.

At the end of the enclosed track keep right and follow a path running with a wall on the right for a short distance, after which the path climbs left to the top of the ridge, passing first over the minor summits of Crug Mawr and

The top of Rhiw Trumau, looking north to Pen Trumau.

Ancient boundary stones on the summit of Pen Twyn Glas.

The track between Pen Twyn Glas and Pen Allt Mawr. The track continues left, from Pen Twyn Glas, to the long ridge of Mynydd Llysiau.

Pen Allt Mawr from the south.

Disgwylfa, and then running with the forest boundary to Pentwynmawr and then Pen y Gadair Fawr.

DISTANCE: 11.25 kilometres (7 miles)
ASCENT: 650 metres (2130 feet)

The continuation north-west to Waun Fach should present no real difficulties beyond the circumnavigation of the wettest ground, but a compass bearing and a more or less direct line is advisable in misty conditions.

DISTANCE: 2 kilometres (1.25 miles)
ASCENT: 75 metres (245 feet)

Route 14.7 The Allt Mawr ridge The Allt Mawr ridge, bounded on the west by the Rhiangoll valley and on the east by the Grwyne Fechan, is superb walking country, affording hours of easy wandering on wide, grassy ridges. Like other ridges in the Black Mountains, the Allt Mawr is much favoured by glider pilots for its up-currents, though they do apparently present problems as I learned from one such pilot I encountered recce-ing the ridge on foot. He confessed to tales of horsemen being unseated by the sudden appearance from below the ridge of the massive, silent form of a glider, and of more than one erstwhile-contented rambler having his hat all but knocked off by a wing tip! Who said the Black Mountains were boring?

Strolling along the ridge will prove delightful to most walkers. Getting on to the ridge in the first place, however, as so often is the case in South Wales, has its problems. For although many footpaths are shown on the various maps, few of them are of any practical use, especially those which approach the ridge from the adjoining valleys.

Route 14.5b describes an ascent across the slopes to join the ridge just north of Mynydd Llysiau (Distance: 2.75 kilometres, 1.7 miles; Ascent: 370 metres, 1215 feet). The same point on the ridge may be reached from Ysgubor Ganol (191270 – not named on the 1:50000 map), by taking the minor road leading south-east to farm build-

A collapsed stone wall defines the way south from Pen Allt Mawr to Pen Cerrig Calch.

ings, but before reaching them keeping left on to a sign-posted track ('To the hill'), which ascends the western flank of Mynydd Llysiau (Distance to Mynydd Llysiau: 3.75 kilometres, 2.3 miles; Ascent: 420 metres, 1380 feet).

The route southwards along the ridge is easy, keeping the steep drop into the upper part of Grwyne Fechan on the left. After the elongated summit of Mynydd Llysiau, the highest point of which is difficult to be precise about, the route crosses a relatively narrow neck of land to reach a pile of ancient boundary stones on Pen Twyn Glas where the path becomes more distinct, veering south-west and then due south to a steep, short pull to the trig point on Pen Allt Mawr. The last noticeable summit south along the ridge, Pen Cerrig Calch, looms in the distance and is best attained by taking a well-defined track along the rim of Cwm Banw – one of the minor side valleys of the Grwyne Fechan. There is another short and steep ascent to reach the trig point on the summit of Pen Cerrig Calch. The distance from Mynydd Llysiau to Pen Cerrig Calch is 6.5 kilometres (4 miles). The ascent travelling south (from the summit of Mynydd Llysiau to that of Pen Cerrig Calch) is 160 metres (525 feet); travelling north it is 130 metres (425 feet).

Reaching Pen Cerrig Calch from the south poses minor problems of route finding, though they are not difficult to resolve. There are two principal ways, both taking in Crug Hywel (Table Mountain), from where the continuation up to Pen Cerrig Calch is both obvious and simple, following a well-tramped path. The ascents to Crug Hywel are described in Route 14.8, since they form pleasant short walks in themselves.

Route 14.8 Crug Hywel (Table Mountain) The Iron-Age hill fort of Crug Hywel, more popularly known as Table Mountain (for fairly obvious reasons), dominates the town of Crickhowell. The fort is thought to have been a fortress of Hywel Dda, the enlightened tenth-century lawgiver who imposed a heavy fine on those who robbed a hawk's nest, and made proper financial provision for women in matrimony. There are two principal routes to its summit, both affording access to the Allt Mawr ridge, and the second route (14.8b) in reverse giving a useful descent to Llanbedr for anyone who has completed the traverse of both the Pen y Gadair Fawr–Waun Fach and Allt Mawr ridges as described in Routes 14.6 and 14.7.

14.8a From Crickhowell Start at the White Hart Inn on the A40 just north-west of the town, and follow a lane ascending steeply on the right of the inn. At the first junction, turn right, and continue to a footpath sign on the left. Cross a stile and take the left edge of a field, with Cwmbeth Brook below. Continue, with a wire fence, to another stile partly concealed by a tree, and then through a

The start of the steep descent into Grwyne Fawr from near the summit of Pen y Gadair Fawr. The hill across the valley is Chwarel y Fan.

gate and over yet another stile into the dingle leading to a metal gate. Cross and follow a stream, later ascending between stone walls to two gates, then make for a sheep pen and follow a stone wall on the right leading to a well-worn path and a further stone wall. From here the northern end of Table Mountain is attainable without difficulty.

DISTANCE: 2.5 kilometres (1.6 miles)
ASCENT: 365 metres (1200 feet)

14.8b From Llanbedr At 235207, a short distance from Llanbedr, a signed footpath and a stile lead into a tree tunnel to an iron gate, and then to a stony track rising to the edge of an open field. Ascend steeply to a gate at the farm buildings above, Perth y Pia, but note that the footpath does not go directly to the buildings, zig-zagging first left and then right, though there is no obvious path anywhere just here.

Pass between the buildings and turn right, then, at the rear of them, turn immediately left and ascend along a field

The patchwork fields below Mynydd Troed. ▶

boundary to another gate. Crug Hywel (Table Mountain) lies directly ahead up grassy slopes that are slippery when wet.

DISTANCE: 1 kilometre (0.6 miles)
ASCENT: 230 metres (755 feet)

The continuation from Crug Hywel to Pen Cerrig Calch is by a clear path ascending the south-eastern slopes.

DISTANCE: 2 kilometres (1.25 miles)
ASCENT: 275 metres (900 feet)

Route 14.9 Mynydd Pen-y-fal (Sugar Loaf) Around the town of Abergavenny are grouped three hills, a well-known endurance walk called The Three Peaks, the highest of which, looking very much from some angles like the heap of sugar poured from a bag that has given rise to its local name, Sugar Loaf, is Mynydd Pen-y-fal. The other two hills are Ysgyryd Fawr (Skirrid Fawr), and Blorenge. In spite of its academic lack of stature, a mere 596 metres (1955 feet), Sugar Loaf always has a feel of being much higher, for it is isolated from the rest of the Black Mountains range and approaches to it can be quite long, though neither of those described here will prove very demanding.

14.9a From Mynydd Llanwenarth This is the shortest ascent of Sugar Loaf, starting from the viewpoint car park at 268167, and taking a clear track curving along the ridge of Mynydd Llanwenarth and up the south-west slope of the hill.

DISTANCE: 2.5 kilometres (1.6 miles)
ASCENT: 250 metres (820 feet)

14.9b From Ffro The ascent from the car park at Ffro on the old Hereford road from Abergavenny to Pant-y-gelli, is only marginally longer than that from Mynydd Llanwenarth, though it is just as easy, taking a well-defined track from the car park (292201) up the north-eastern slopes to the summit.

DISTANCE: 2.75 kilometres (1.7 miles)
ASCENT: 340 metres (1115 feet)

Route 14.10 Mynydd Troed This rather isolated summit, rising above patchwork fields in the valleys below, is an excellent viewpoint, and its ascent is unlikely to take anyone much more than forty minutes or so. For walkers wanting a slightly longer day, Mynydd Troed may be combined with the lower summit, Mynydd Llangorse, to the south-west without unduly taxing navigational expertise.

For Mynydd Troed start from a small parking area at 161284 at the head of Cwm Sorgwm where there are three small stones marking the boundaries of three nineteenth-century landowners. From here there are well-worn paths leading both north to Mynydd Troed, and south-west to Mynydd Llangorse.

DISTANCE: 1 kilometre (0.6 miles)
ASCENT: 255 metres (835 feet)

Route 14.11 The Cat's Back ridge and Black Hill The whole of this ridge and mountain on the north-eastern side of the Olchon valley are in England, though, as part of the Black Mountains range, they are included for completeness (and because it would be daft to leave them out!). The route described here may easily be combined with a continuation to Hay Bluff and Black Mountain, descending along part of Offa's Dyke Path.

Start from the car park at 288328, just to the north-west of Little Black Hill, and take the signposted path 'Black Hill and Offa's Dyke Path'. Cross the stile and climb the slope to reach the ridge above, where the gradient eases. The ridge soon becomes a series of rocky steps passing between the two lines of crags shown on the 1:50 000 map, and climbing to a cairn near some old quarry workings. Narrowing for a short distance, the ridge then broadens into Black Hill, the summit of which is marked by a trig point.

DISTANCE: 2.5 kilometres (1.6 miles)

ASCENT: 275 metres (900 feet)

There is a well-worn path leading north-westwards to Hay Bluff, passing around the head of the Olchon valley.

Section 15 – Brecon Beacons

	MAP REFERENCE	HEIGHT (m)	1:50 000 OS MAP
Pen y Fan	012216	886	160
Corn Du	007213	873	160
Cribyn	024213	795	160
Waun Rydd	062206	769	160
Gwaun Cerrig Llwydion	055204	754	160
Unnamed summit (Fan y Big)	042197	730	160
Fan y Big	036207	719	160
Allt Lwyd	079189	654	160
Y Gyrn	989216	619	160
Cefn yr Ystrad	087137	617	160

ROUTES

15.1 Pen y Fan and Corn Du from the Storey Arms

15.2 Pen y Fan by the north ridge

15.3 Corn Du through Cwm Llwch

15.4 Corn Du from Taf Fechan

15.5 Cribyn from Taf Fechan

15.6 Cribyn by Bryn Teg, the north ridge

15.7 Fan y Big by Cefn Cyff, the north ridge

15.8 Waun Rydd from Talybont

15.9 Waun Rydd from Llanfrynach

From all directions, and for many miles around, even from as far as Radnor Forest, the distinctive flat-topped summits of the Brecon Beacons are instantly recognisable. (The Isle of Skye is the only other place in Britain with comparable flattened hills.) Their graceful simplicity of line is at once alluring and beguiling. Seen in an evening light the sweeping shapes of Pen y Fan and Corn Du send richly purple shadows into the depths of Cwm Llwch, while in the dawn these same hills appear icy cold above a distant blue haze.

Pen y Fan, Corn Du and Cribyn are the main attraction for hill-walkers, their popularity causing scarred tracks across the hills visible for miles and which will last for decades. Yet there are many more hills in the Beacons that are equally worthy of attention, and just as easy to ascend. The whole area, for the purposes of this book, is roughly triangular, following the line of the A470 from Brecon to the Heads of the Valleys road (A465), and then along the shores of the Pontsticill and Talybont reservoirs to the village of Talybont (113228 – on Sheet 161), where it follows the southern edge of Llangorse Lake. Within this area lie ten summits over 600 metres in height, all well worth visiting, all affording enjoyable walking. But as experienced walkers will deduce, there are, in this kind of simple, unassuming terrain, problems that are not readily apparent. The very simplicity is one in itself; there are few identifiable features on which to take bearings, and the mists roll across the landscape unhindered. Smooth, clean shapes offer little resistance to wind, rain and snow, and in winter these hills are treacherous for the unwary. With long northern ridges, a descent into the wrong valley can mean an arduous trudge at the end of the day. But on a clear, fair day with buzzards and gliders sharing the air the sheer grandeur of the Beacons is unsurpassed in the whole of South Wales.

Route 15.1 Pen y Fan and Corn Du from the Storey Arms This ascent to the highest summit in South Wales is simple and uncomplicated, being along a wide, eroded path all the way to the summit. It is, as a result, far less rewarding than the ascents by the long northern ridges, and by no means as dramatic.

Just over half a kilometre south-east of the Storey Arms Youth Adventure Centre, a short way beyond a wooden

toilet block (987198), a path runs for a short distance through the edge of a small forest to a wooden kissing gate. After the gate descend, right, to cross a stream, the Blaen Taf Fawr, and continue on a wide ascending track passing en route a column denoting the generosity of the Eagle Star Insurance Company in giving this part of the Brecon Beacons to the National Trust.

The track ascends to, and crosses, Bwlch Duwynt, just south of Corn Du (to which an easy diversion up a series of rocky steps may be made), and continues directly to the summit of Pen y Fan. This is the easiest ascent of an 800-metre summit in the whole of Wales, but continuation from Pen y Fan to the adjoining mountain, Cribyn, or to descend by Pen y Fan's north ridge requires care in misty conditions in order to find the correct line down the steep north and east faces. A return to Corn Du, however, presents no such difficulty, the steep north face in this instance, kept on one's right hand, clearly defines the way. Even so, care is required in winter when the whole line of these northern faces can become heavily corniced. Viewed from below in winter weather it can look as formidable today as it did in March 1188 to that fast-moving, fast-talking cleric, Gerald the Welshman, as he toted the Archbishop of Canterbury round Wales to drum up support for the Third Crusade. Gerald explains the name the connecting saddle between Pen y Fan and Corn Du still bears today: "Cadair Arthur, or Arthur's Chair, so called from two peaks which rise up in the form of a throne. This summit is a very lofty spot and most difficult of access, so that in the minds of simple folk it is thought to have belonged to Arthur, the greatest and most distinguished King of the Britons."

The summit of Pen y Fan, now rather more eroded than

▲ *Pen y Fan and Corn Du, from Cwm Llwch.*

◄ *The high summits of the Brecon Beacons seen from the ridge to Fan y Big.*

Gerald of Wales might have found it had he ascended to it, is marked by a trig point; Corn Du by a large cairn.
DISTANCE: 3 kilometres (1.9 miles)
ASCENT: 450 metres (1475 feet)

Route 15.2 Pen y Fan by the north ridge The main summits of the Brecon Beacons are all blessed with long northern ridges which provide enjoyable walking of no great difficulty. This ascent of Pen y Fan is no exception until the very end when a final steep section has to be tackled.

The route starts from a car park in Cwm Gwdi (026248), and takes a signposted footpath over a stile, across a bridge, and then by steps and a way-marked path across the shoulder of the minor top, Allt Du. As the lower part of the north ridge is approached the track tends to peter out, but becomes clear again on the ascent of the main section of the ridge, here named Cefn Cwm Llwch. Thereafter the route follows a path along the top of the ridge to the final steep pull to the summit. This upper section is badly eroded and can present difficulties in winter or other wet conditions.

An alternative start may be made from the car park by crossing the stile, near the gate, at the end of the metalled roadway. This route goes by a broad track through former MOD Rifle Ranges, no longer used by the Army, and though rocky and rough in places is clear to follow and without difficulty, joining the above route at Cefn Cwm Llwch.
DISTANCE: 3.5 kilometres (2.2 miles)
ASCENT: 600 metres (1970 feet)

Route 15.3 Corn Du through Cwm Llwch The ascent of Corn Du through the wide and beautiful valley of Cwm

The Milan Ridge ascending to Corn Du. ▲

The Tommy Jones' Monument on the Milan Ridge. ▶

Llwch is a refreshing experience, and is a simple walk without difficulty.

The route starts alongside the stream, Nant Cwm Llwch, at 006245, where at the end of a stony road there is an unexpected area of open grassland and plenty of room to park cars. A wide path starts off south, heading into Cwm Llwch and crosses a shallow ford by a bridge before ascending a little to Cwm Llwch Farm, now used as a schools' project centre. The path is diverted, right, around the farm, then continues clearly to the boundary, at a stile, of the Brecon Beacons National Park.

Just beyond the stile the path rises sharply for a short distance, and then climbs more gently to a hollow formed by glacial moraine in which reposes Llyn Cwm Llwch, a beautiful lake, which could easily, and undeservedly, be missed by walkers keeping to the well-blazed track. Like many lakes in Wales Llyn Cwm Llwch is reputedly bottomless, some even maintaining that there is a subterranean link with Llangorse Lake some distance to the east. There are stories of fairies and treasure and of a gigantic man who once threatened to drown the whole valley of the Usk if his peace was disturbed. For this reason it may be wise to pass Llyn Cwm Llwch quietly.

The track by-passing the lake, now showing signs of erosion, climbs above it to gain the edge of the cwm's western shoulder, near to an obelisk commemorating the tragedy of five-year-old Tommy Jones. Tommy Jones set out from Brecon with his father in 1900 to visit relatives living at Cwm Llwch Farm. At a place known locally as the Logan, not far from journey's end, they stopped at a military camp for a drink, and were soon joined by Tommy's grandfather and his cousin. The two boys were sent on to the farm, but en route Tommy became afraid – it is a very lonely and fearsome spot for a child of five – and began to retrace his steps to the Logan. He never arrived. When the alarm was raised a search was carried out all through the night and for many days afterwards, until, quite by chance, Tommy's body was found a month later

On the summit of Corn Du.

1300 feet above the valley on the ridge, known as the Milan ridge, leading up to Corn Du where he had died of exhaustion. Even as I was researching for this book friends at Libanus, down in the river valley, were still expressing amazement that a child of five could ever have managed to reach the spot where he perished.

From the obelisk, but for which Tommy Jones would be forgotten, a track continues along the Milan ridge keeping to the edge of the cwm, above Craig Cwm Llwch, to ascend finally and steeply to the summit of Corn Du. Typically this final section is eroded and potentially dangerous, while to describe parts of the summit plateau as a morass is flattering only to deceive. Photographers will find that the northern edge of the plateau gives a very impressive view of the route of ascent, Llyn Cwm Llwch far below, and of nearby Pen y Fan.

DISTANCE: 4 kilometres (2.5 miles)
ASCENT: 600 metres (1970 feet)

Route 15.4 Corn Du from Taf Fechan From Blaen Taf Fechan (035174) continue along the metalled roadway to the waterworks buildings at the Lower Neuadd reservoir, and join a track which ascends, left, along the northern edge of the forest to gain a broad ridge near the minor summit, Twyn Mwyalchod (022176). Continue north along this ridge with a splendid prospect, right, of the Upper Neuadd reservoir, and climb gently, across a narrowing of the ridge at Rhiw yr Ysgyfarnog to the unmarked top of Craig Gwaun Taf.

A short descent northwards leads to Bwlch Duwynt, meeting the main track from the Storey Arms to Pen y Fan (Route 15.1), which should be crossed to a rising flight of rocky steps on to the boggy summit plateau of Corn Du.
DISTANCE: 6 kilometres (3.75 miles)
ASCENT: 475 metres (1560 feet)

This route, extended to cover Pen y Fan and Cribyn, and linked with Route 15.5 in reverse (not as difficult as it sounds!), will make a satisfying round trip of 12 kilometres (7.5 miles).

Route 15.5 Cribyn from Taf Fechan A Roman road passes through Cwm Cynwyn and continues south into the Taf Fechan Forest at the northern end of the Pontsticill reservoir where the Forestry Commission has constructed parking places and toilets. The road, now only a rough track, may be joined conveniently at Blaen Taf Fechan (035174), from where it is easy to follow to its highest point, the Cwm Cynwyn gap, at the col between Cribyn and Fan y Big (this latter mountain being named only on the 1:10 000 map. Big here is Welsh, not English, meaning *beak*). This track through the gap was the original bridleway from Brecon to Merthyr Tydfil, and must have been a desolate route in the depths of winter. The main summits of the Beacons, Cribyn, Pen y Fan and, beyond, Corn Du, are in view throughout this approach, as it climbs gently above the tree-flanked tranquillity of the Upper Neuadd reservoir.

Pen y Fan, the highest summit in South Wales, and Cribyn, from Corn Du.

From the col a steep path ascends, left, to the summit of Cribyn, while an easier path contours around on the south side to the col between Cribyn and Pen y Fan – not that the ascent of Cribyn from that side is any less of a grind.

DISTANCE: 4.5 kilometres (2.8 miles)
ASCENT: 370 metres (1210 feet)

This route may also be used to make an ascent from the south of Fan y Big involving a steep ascent to it, right, from the Cwm Cynwyn gap. South of Fan y Big (unhelpfully without a name on most maps) lies a genuinely unnamed summit at 042197 with which Fan y Big may easily be combined. A random descent, south-west, from 042197 will lead easily back to the Roman road.

DISTANCE: 3.75 kilometres (2.4 miles)
ASCENT: 290 metres (950 feet)

Route 15.6 Cribyn by Bryn Teg, the north ridge Like those of adjacent Pen y Fan and Fan y Big the north ridge of Cribyn provides easy walking. In common also with those ridges it is difficult to get to without a car, starting at the northern end (at 037237) of the Roman road passing from Taf Fechan to the south through Cwm Cynwyn. The nearest identifiable feature is the farm, Bailea (041241), most easily reached along a pleasant minor road running due south from Llanfaes in Brecon.

From the end of the metalled roadway, just south of Bailea, where with a certain amount of difficulty a few cars could be parked, a stony track leads to a gate letting on to open pasture. At this point the Roman road tracks left across the flank of the north ridge (Bryn Teg), but a wide, grassy track can be seen making directly up the ridge. This track later deteriorates into a narrow path and continues between two small pools (that look as though they will dry up in prolonged hot weather) to the foot of a final steep section climbing to the summit cairn. This last section is now badly eroded, and requires great care at all times, especially in winter conditions.

From the foot of the final steep section a track goes to the right, across the north face of Cribyn, to the col between Cribyn and Pen y Fan. This is also badly eroded, and in three places caution is required in both wet *and* dry conditions.

DISTANCE: 3 kilometres (1.9 miles)
ASCENT: 465 metres (1525 feet)

Route 15.7 Fan y Big by Cefn Cyff, the north ridge Of the four northern ridges emanating from the main summits of the Brecon Beacons, the easterly two, Cefn Cyff and Gist Wen, are less dramatic than the others, though they provide equally easy and enjoyable walking, with the possibility of combining the two ridges to make a long walk from the village of Llanfrynach (075256). Ironically this requires greater map-reading skill on the roads and small lanes leading to and from the village than on the mountains.

The ascent of Cefn Cyff starts at Pen yr Heol (057241 –

not named on the 1:50000 map), though there is neither room to park nor turn cars. The route passes through a blue iron gate on to a rising stony track leading to a wooden gate. The view from the gate is magnificent, especially in summer when the patchwork fields below provide a contrasting pattern of colour rolling away to the Black Mountains on the border with England.

Beyond the gate the track is obvious as it climbs the steepest part of the ridge, and remains largely uninteresting until Pen y Fan, Cribyn and finally Fan y Big come into view, with a widening prospect, left, across Cwm Oergwm. The path along the top of the ridge is narrow, but remains clear throughout its length. Care, however, should be taken in misty conditions as the ground rises because the path does not actually cross the highest point.

The path continues south and south-east to the unnamed summit at 042197.

DISTANCE: 4 kilometres (2.5 miles)
ASCENT: 430 metres (1410 feet)

Cribyn, showing the track across its north face. This track is dangerous in a few places, especially in winter.

There is an interesting and pleasant alternative start to this route, beginning in the village of Llanfrynach. Near Tyfry Farm (073258) a signposted bridleway (denoted by a small blue arrow on a white square, and clearly marked on the 1:50000 map) leads through a wooden kissing gate and along the edge of a field. Signs are infrequent and not easily seen, but as a guide stay close to the river until, at a rickety iron gate (that isn't going to last for ever!), a signpost finally points away from it. This then gives a short uphill climb to emerge from the trees which have decorated the route so far. At the edge of the wood another sign points diagonally left across a field to a gate and a more obvious track along a hedgerow leading to Tynllwyn Farm (063247). The track continues through the farmyard and on to a metalled roadway, leading in a short distance to a junction. At this junction go left, and, later, at a fork, *ignore* a turning signposted to Pen Twyn. Instead keep right and ascend past the entrance to Rhiwiau and so to the right turn at the entrance to Pen yr Heol.

DISTANCE: 2.5 kilometres (1.6 miles)
ASCENT: 170 metres (560 feet)

The walk around the rim of Cwm Oergwm is easy, and gives good retrospective views of the main Brecon summits.

Route 15.8 Waun Rydd from Talybont Waun Rydd is an elongated plateau of boggy moorland to the east of Fan y Big, the main attraction of which lies in the easiness of the walking to be found there. Little else will be found of interest, but walkers who enjoy quiet moorland wandering will find the route described here, a circular tour in fact, a worthwhile change from the touristy treks up and down the more popular summits of the Brecon Beacons.

The route starts at a convenient lay-by at 099196 (on Sheet 161). Opposite the lay-by a gate leads into Forestry Commission land along a metalled surface which is abandoned after about 200 metres by crossing a stile on the right, at a footpath sign. A grassy track now ascends through bracken to a second stile at a gate. This leads on to open hillside with forest on the left. Ascend ahead and then climb left to the edge of the forest until the end of the forest is reached. Here go left, south, for a short distance along the forest edge and then start to ascend right, west again, through tussock grass, peat and bilberries, to the unmarked summit of Allt Lwyd.

Descend north-west on a path across a narrow ridge and climb easily to the edge of the plateau of Waun Rydd. The trig point does not mark the highest point, which lies almost one kilometre (0.6 miles) further to the north-west.

Return from the summit to the path passing near the trig point and follow this east to a large cairn, Cairn Pica, on the edge of the plateau, and descend steeply at first along the ridge of Twyn Du. There is a good path across the whole of this lower section, but as it approaches more forest the path becomes lost in bracken and it is necessary to take a bearing on the dam of the reservoir until the track re-appears at a stile. Once across the stile, and descending through undergrowth, watch for a track going right across a small stream. Thereafter the track is narrow but clear and descends quickly, finally turning left to join the road to Berthllwyd Farm at a footpath sign (103208). The road continues ahead for a short distance to join the main road near Aber

village, where a right turn will lead back to the lay-by.
DISTANCE: 11 kilometres (6.9 miles)
ASCENT: 570 metres (1870 feet)

Route 15.9 Waun Rydd from Llanfrynach From Llanfrynach take the minor road running south-west from
075255 and ascend this to a gate, on the left, opposite the
second entrance to Tregaer Farm (072249). Pass through
the gate and follow an enclosed track to another gate, after
which there is a short drop to a ford. Across the ford go left
and then almost immediately right to climb along a fence-
line of trees and shrubs to the vicinity of the ruin, Tir Hir
(075246 – not named on the 1:50000 map). As you
approach Tir Hir it is possible to bear diagonally right
across the field to another gate, after which a path meanders upwards through trees to a final gate. Beyond the last
gate, climb steeply for a short distance to join a broad track

The upper reaches of Cwm Oergwm.

beneath the minor summit, Bryn. This track should then be followed until, as it steepens, it is possible to ascend directly to the summit of Waun Rydd. Alternatively the steep ascent to the summit may be eased by staying on the rising track to an obvious col, at which turn sharp left along a track (not shown on maps – and which eventually leads to Talybont), but leave this after about half a kilometre and climb over rough ground to the summit.

DISTANCE: 6 kilometres (3.75 miles)
ASCENT: 650 metres (2130 feet)

It is possible to make a 12.5 kilometres (8 miles) circular walk and have a long and satisfying day out by following the path south-west below Waun Rydd, round the rim of Cwm Oergwm, and descending Route 15.7 in reverse, down Cefn Cyff to Pen yr Heol (057241), and then back to Llanfrynach by the alternative start to that route.

Llyn Cwm Llwch, claimed to be inhabited by a gigantic man who threatens to drown the valley of the Usk if his peace is disturbed.

Section 16 – Mynydd Du and Fforest Fawr

	MAP REFERENCE	HEIGHT (m)	1:50 000 OS MAP
Ban Brycheiniog	825218	802	160
Fan Hir	831209	761	160
Picws Du (Bannau Sir Gaer)	812218	749	160
Fan Fawr	970193	734	160
Fan Gihirych	881191	725	160
Fan Fraith	887184	668	160
Fan Nedd	913184	663	160
Garreg Las	777203	635	160
Fan Llia	938186	632	160
Fan Frynych	958228	629	160
Unnamed summit (Craig Cerrig-gleisiad)	961218	629	160
Garreg Lwyd	741179	619	160
Fan Dringarth	941193	617	160
Fan Bwlch Chwyth	912216	603	160
Foel Fraith	757183	602	160

ROUTES

16.1 Garreg Lwyd and Foel Fraith from Pen Rhiw Wen
16.2 Picws Du (Bannau Sir Gaer) from Llanddeusant
16.3 Ban Brycheiniog and Fan Hir by Llyn y Fan Fawr and Bwlch y Giedd
16.4 Fan Hir from Tafarn y Garreg
16.5 Fan Gihirych from Bwlch Bryn Rhudd
16.6 Fan Nedd from Maen Llia
16.7 Fan Llia and Fan Dringarth from Blaen Llia
16.8 Fan Fawr from the Storey Arms

The very names, Mynydd Du (*Black Mountain*) and Fforest Fawr (*Great Forest*), speak of wilderness and desolation, a description with some basis in reality, if not quite so starkly as the imagination may conjure up. They are names of a vast area of upland, infrequently visited (certainly by comparison with the over-populated Brecon Beacons to the east) where a true feeling of isolation still prevails. Stretching from the minor top, Tair Carn Uchaf

(694173) in the west, a convoluted grassy ridge, crossed only by three north-to-south roads, twists and turns eastwards for 32 kilometres (20 miles) to the massive dome of Fan Fawr (970193), gazing phlegmatically at the flat-topped, trampled Beacons.

The most prominent feature of Mynydd Du is the long escarpment running north from Glyntawe to the highest summit, Ban Brycheiniog, where it turns west to present its steep face to the rolling moorland which lies to the north. The complete traverse of this escarpment, known locally as Carmarthan Fan, from Tafarn y Garreg to far-off Llanddeusant is a tremendously rewarding experience with ever-changing views and a splendid sense of elevation, as much spiritual as physical. Nor does anything compare in the whole of South Wales with the idyllic, almost romantic setting of the two lakes, Llyn y Fan Fawr and Llyn y Fan Fach. Indeed the latter is reputedly the home of the Lady of the Lake, who fell in love with a local farm lad living at nearby Blaen Sawdde.

Near Llyn y Fan Fawr rises the source of the river Tawe, while the northern escarpment turns its waters to the Usk, a river which now divides the counties of Powys and Dyfed, and from the banks of which the Carmarthen Fan is seen most vividly in stormy or early evening light.

Fforest Fawr is not a forest in the modern sense of a dense area of trees, it is the medieval usage, which described any tract of uncultivated wild land reserved for hunting. It was the first Lord of Brecon, Bernard de Neufmarche, who established Fforest Fawr. Under the Normans the Marcher Lords could have whatever land they could hold. By the thirteenth century a further forest, Fforest Fechan, had been added, incorporating into an arena for medieval entertainment much of the mountainous country between Storey Arms and the river Tawe, and beyond to the long ridge, Fan Hir. Even now it may look very much to us as it appeared to the Lords of Brecon.

The whole area of Fforest Fawr is worthy of exploration not only because it includes a range of domed, grassy hills

Fan Gihirych, one of the summits on Cnewr Estate land in Fforest Fawr.

that are generally easy to negotiate and pleasant to walk, but also for its geological significance, being on the edge of carboniferous limestone country with its numerous caves and potholes. The most famous and accessible of the caves are the Dan yr Ogof near Glyntawe, which provide an entertaining and well-presented underground excursion. But many of the hills are riddled with subterranean passages and waterways that have long fascinated the serious potholer.

Route 16.1 Garreg Lwyd and Foel Fraith from Pen Rhiw Wen
Possessing not only the distinction of being the most westerly 600-metre summit in South Wales, but also that of one of the most easily ascended – vying for that particular accolade with Hay Bluff in the Black Mountains, and

the unnamed summit at the head of Rhondda Fawr – Garreg Lwyd is a mountain likely to appeal only to walkers in search of trackless solitude. Yet this bleak rock-strewn summit, looking very much as if its Maker in the act of creation had taken a tea break and forgotten to resume the task, displays a certain charm, and boasts views extending as far as Swansea, Port Talbot, the Gower Peninsula and, to the east, the Brecon Beacons whose decapitated tops peer across Bwlch y Giedd between the long ridge of Fan Hir and the higher Ban Brycheiniog.

The summit, identified by a white painted trig point and a curious circular configuration of stone shelters, is most easily achieved by ascending on a line of one's own choosing across grass and rock from Pen Rhiw Wen (731185) at the top of the A4069. There is no path, nor is one needed on an ascent over which even the most dilatory walkers would be hard pressed to expend more than thirty minutes.

DISTANCE: 1 kilometre (0.6 miles)
ASCENT: 120 metres (395 feet)

The continuation to Foel Fraith is very much a walk on the wild side, crossing desolate peat moorland and offering a delectable and quite unexpected area of tranquillity, so close to civilisation.

The summit, on a peaty plateau, is marked by a cairn of large stones.

DISTANCE: 1.75 kilometres (1.1 miles)
ASCENT: 90 metres (295 feet)

Route 16.2 Picws Du (Bannau Sir Gaer) from Llanddeusant The Youth Hostel at Llanddeusant (777245) is an ideal starting point for a short, pleasing walk to one of the most imposing mountains in South Wales, Picws Du, *Black Peak*, better known perhaps as Bannau Sir Gaer. Like the other summits of the Carmarthen Fan, Bannau Sir Gaer possesses a steep escarpment face, dropping regally to the valley below in which reclines the jewel of

Llyn y Fan Fach, a most eye-catching lake particularly when the rays of the late afternoon sun spill across the rim of the surrounding cliffs to transform the surface of the lake into shimmering diamonds.

At other times Llyn y Fan Fach is a sombre, mysterious lake in a wild setting, sheltered, still and silent save for the herds of wild ponies that frequent these hills and the occasional mewing of a buzzard circling overhead. It was, so legend tells us, on a rock by the edge of the lake that a farming lad from nearby Blaen Sawdde first encountered one of the Celtic Fairy Folk, the Tylwyth Teg, tales of whom so often decorate the history of Wales. The Lady of the Lake, as she became known, promised, after a certain amount of wooing, to be the lad's bride providing her father consented. On his next visit to the lake the lad was met by a man accompanied by five identical maidens, his daughters, and was asked to pick out the right girl. Even in legend feminine ingenuity has its place for, not to be deprived of her suitor, the Lady of the Lake gave him a sign with her toe so that he would recognise her. By so doing not only could the lad have his bride, but also as many sheep and cattle as he could count. Predictably there was a catch – if at any time he touched his wife with iron she would instantly return to the lake with her dowry. Of course, fairy stories being what they are, the inevitable happened, and after many years of happy marriage the Lady returned to her lake where, presumably, though the ending of the tale varies, she may repose to this day.

To reach this lake with its mysterious tale leave Llanddeusant by the narrow road running east from the church, following signs to Llyn y Fan, and as the road enters the land owned by the Welsh Water Authority turn left to continue along a rough, stony track which runs alongside the bubbling river Sawdde and climbs to filter beds. The view of Bannau Sir Gaer opens up ahead, appearing from this angle as the black, pointed peak of its other name and seeming to dominate everything around it. You can reach the filter beds by car, but to do so takes away a good deal of the pleasure afforded by a more relaxed, pedestrian approach.

Beyond the filter beds the track continues rising gently until it suddenly reaches the beautiful mountain setting in which Llyn y Fan Fach is the centrepiece. Bannau Sir Gaer rises impressively on the left, but the way to it is in the opposite direction, ascending west, up and around the shoulder of Tyle Gwyn on a clear path keeping close to the edge of the escarpment all the way to the summit. The top of the mountain, marked by a large cairn, is a relaxing place to be on a warm day, commanding a panoramic view, especially to the south and west, in which the Gower Peninsula figures prominently.

DISTANCE: 7 kilometres (4.4 miles)
ASCENT: 490 metres (1605 feet)

By descending steeply eastwards from the summit to the col before the ascent to Ban Brycheiniog, a track twisting down and then across the escarpment provides an alternative return to the lake.

Route 16.3 Ban Brycheiniog and Fan Hir by Llyn y Fan Fawr and Bwlch y Giedd On a hot summer's day the ascent from the east of Ban Brycheiniog has two distinct advantages. The mountain may be ascended with relative ease, starting along the banks of the cascading river Tawe, followed by a short stretch of open moorland and then by an obvious rising track to Bwlch y Giedd. Llyn y Fan Fawr is a superbly inviting lake, reflecting myriad hues of blue and green and coaxing even the most die-hard non-swimmers like myself to take the plunge. In winter, however, one may be excused if the subtlety of Llyn y Fan Fawr's summer captivation is not readily appreciated.

Just below the summit of the Glyntawe to Trecastell road, and about 300 metres beyond the stile giving access to the prominent standing stone, a narrow path (starting at 853218) heads westwards towards the source of the river Tawe. The path is not immediately obvious, but a bee-line for the river, crossing first the small tributary coming down from the north, will soon disclose it running along the river's true left bank, and provide a most enjoyable start to the walk as it flirts with the twists and turns and tumbling falls. After little more than a kilometre cross the river and ascend over open moorland above which peer the long ridge of Fan Hir and the rugged face of Ban Brycheiniog. There are no prominent tracks across this short stretch of moorland, but the col between the two mountains, Bwlch y Giedd, is an easy target and will lead to the southern end of Llyn y Fan Fawr. From the lake the continuation to Bwlch y Giedd, by a prominent scarred track, now loose scree in places, is easily gained. I once sat on this track watching an otter obviously enjoying a swim across the mirror-smooth surface of the lake; shortly

Fan Fawr, from the Storey Arms path to Pen y Fan.

afterwards I decided to take swimming lessons – there is always something to be learned from nature!

A new fence has been erected up to Bwlch y Giedd, and from it neither the ascent, left, to Fan Hir (the summit of which is unmarked), or, right, to Ban Brycheiniog, should take more than ten minutes. The highest point of Ban Brycheiniog boasts a trig point and a neat circular stone shelter, both close to the edge of the escarpment dropping steeply into the lake below. A better vantage point, however, may be found a short distance further north on the minor top, Twr y Fan Foel (824221), when the next summit, Picws Du (Bannau Sir Gaer), and the patchwork fields and moorland to the north come suddenly into view.

DISTANCE: 4 kilometres (2.5 miles)
ASCENT: 405 metres (1330 feet)

The land north of Fan Fawr in Fforest Fawr is bleak and barren, and there are few landmarks of any use in misty conditions.

From Twr y Fan Foel a progressively steepening descent south-west leads along the edge of the northern escarpment to the col below Picws Du (Bannau Sir Gaer) from where it is a short steep pull to the summit cairn, and a splendid prospect of Llyn y Fan Fach, if anything an even more tempting lake than its compatriot beneath Ban Brycheiniog, surrounded by steep cliffs. This is the legendary home of the Lady of the Lake, one of the Tylwyth Teg, or Fairy Folk (see Route 16.2).

DISTANCE: 1.5 kilometres (1 mile)
ASCENT: 90 metres (295 feet)

Route 16.4 Fan Hir from Tafarn y Garreg The once-popular route from the Gwyn Arms Hotel has now been obscured by road improvements, and has been allowed to become overgrown. There is, however, an acceptable alternative, though both routes involve a hard grind up steep grassy slopes before the southern end of Fan Hir, *Long Ridge*, is reached. With the advantage of starting and finishing at an hotel, walkers may well feel that an ascent over Fan Hir to Ban Brycheiniog and a return down the beautiful Tawe valley has something to commend it!

Alongside the Tafarn y Garreg Hotel car park a sign-posted footpath (Llwybr Cyhoeddus) leads to a wooden bridge (not shown on the 1:50000 map) across the river Tawe, and for a short distance the route is marked by small yellow arrows painted on wooden posts. From the bridge the path runs, against the flow of the stream, through a pleasant setting much favoured by Dippers and Grey Wagtails. After about 200 metres take a gate, left, and follow a rough track to another gate where a right turn leads, after only a few metres, to an iron gate giving on to the open hillside. Follow the path, right, beneath trees until it is possible to ascend, left, very steeply, picking a way through bracken and rocks to gain the southern end of the Fan Hir ridge. By comparison, it is then a simple matter to continue northwards across the unmarked summit, with ever-widening views prominent among which,

The summit trig point on Ban Brycheiniog, with Llyn y Fan Fawr below.

and much nearer at hand, is the deep blue eye of Llyn y Fan Fawr.

DISTANCE: 4 kilometres (2.5 miles)
ASCENT: 540 metres (1770 feet)

The continuation northwards towards Ban Brycheiniog crosses first the high-level pass, Bwlch y Giedd, and then picks up an ascending path leading to the summit of the higher mountain.

DISTANCE: 1 kilometre (0.6 miles)
ASCENT: 100 metres (330 feet)

Route 16.5 Fan Gihirych from Bwlch Bryn Rhudd Fan Gihirych lies within the boundaries of the Cnewr Estate and is not freely accessible. The Estate will allow walkers to cross the main summit, but permission must be sought from the Estate Office at Sennybridge, Brecon, LD3 8SP.

Large parties must direct their request to the Brecon Beacons National Park Office at Glamorgan Street, Brecon, LD3 7DP.

It is important to note that access will not be given for the period 15th April to 10th May each year, during the lambing season. The Estate will also be closed at times of high fire risk, when notices will be posted. There is, however, a right of way all the year round, running through the southern part of the Estate land from Penwyllt (855157).

Access to Fan Gihirych is by the following agreed route; it is not marked and it is not intended to mark it.

From a lay-by on the A4067 at Bwlch Bryn Rhudd (870195) cross a stile and ascend very steeply past a tree to

The view south from Twr y Fan Foel reveals a splendid prospect of Ban Brycheiniog and Fan Hir.

gain marginally easier ground with the top of Fan Gihirych looming above. A direct line should be taken for the summit, gaining it by another very steep pull ending abruptly, to reveal the summit trig point standing only 50 metres away across a stretch of tussock grass. The view westwards reveals the long ridge of Fan Hir leading, after the dip to Bwlch y Giedd, on to Ban Brycheiniog, while eastwards, across the intervening bulk of Fan Nedd (also on Cnewr land) peer the familiar decapitated summits of the Brecon Beacons.

The return to the start point in the lay-by is by the same route.

DISTANCE: 1 kilometre (0.6 miles)
ASCENT: 355 metres (1165 feet)

Llyn y Fan Fach, a legendary site of the Lady of the Lake, one of the Tylwyth Teg, or Fairy Folk.

The continuation to Fan Nedd to the east follows an indistinct path along a wide, descending ridge until a new Estate road is encountered. This winds across a narrow and windy neck of land, Bwlch y Duwynt, and leads eventually to a gate across the road. Turn right immediately after the gate and descend along the line of a fence to the col with Fan Nedd from where it is yet another steep grind to a windswept top.

DISTANCE: 4 kilometres (2.5 miles)
ASCENT: 170 metres (555 feet)

Route 16.6 Fan Nedd from Maen Llia The access restraints applying to the ascent of Fan Gihirych apply equally in the case of Fan Nedd; both mountains are on Cnewr Estate land, and access is limited, but will in the main be given. The details for Route 16.5 indicate the approaches that should be made.

The agreed line of ascent starts in the vicinity of the large standing stone, Maen Llia (924193), and enters Cnewr land at either of the two iron gates nearby. There are no paths to follow, and the going is rough and steep, but there is a splendid view from the summit making the ascent well worthwhile.

DISTANCE: 1.5 kilometres (1 mile)
ASCENT: 215 metres (705 feet)

The continuation to Fan Gihirych is straightforward, descending steeply north-west to gain a new Estate access road at Bwlch y Duwynt, and later, as the Estate road swings south, left, leaving it and ascending along the edge of Fan Gihirych's steep northern face to the trig point on the summit.

Route 16.7 Fan Llia and Fan Dringarth from Blaen Llia Fan Llia is one of those summits you can leave for a day when only a gentle stroll is called for, though it is well worth including in a traverse of the hills of Mynydd Du and Fforest Fawr in either direction. The Afon Llia, a

popular place on hot sunny days, was once all that separated the grassy bulk of Fan Llia from the equally grassy,
equally bulky Fan Nedd to the west, a distinction it now
has to share with a minor roadway and encroaching picnic
areas. One such picnic area, provided by the Forestry
Commission, lies towards the southern end of the river at
Blaen Llia and provides an acceptable starting point for an
easy ascent. Typical of many South Wales hills, however,
is the need to spend more time at low levels deciding how
to get on to the hills than will actually be spent climbing
them – or so it seems!

From the picnic area return a short way along the access
to cross a concrete bridge over the river, but do not then
follow the graded forestry track rising to the right. Instead
turn left along the river bank to two stiles across fences.
Beyond one stile there is a very clear rising track, but this
less direct route should be shunned in favour of an indistinct path keeping close to the river for about 100 metres
until it passes through a dilapidated wooden gate. Once
through the gate climb steeply, right, to reach a track
ascending ahead and then left on to the Fan Llia ridge.
The summit is marked by a small group of stones.

DISTANCE: 2.5 kilometres (1.6 miles)
ASCENT: 265 metres (870 feet)

It is worth continuing northwards for a short distance
(without significant ascent) to the unmarked minor summit, Fan Dringarth, and then descending, left, on a track
(if it can be found – though it matters not if it can't!)
making for the upper reaches of the Afon Llia. A good
guide is to take a bearing on the standing stone, Maen Llia
(924193), and to head for this. In any case a diversion to
this prehistoric monolith is of interest in itself. It stands

The peaceful waters of Llyn y Fan Fawr. ▶

Picws Du, Black Peak, *is probably better known as Bannau Sir Gaer.* ▶▶

twelve feet high, nine feet wide and about two and a half feet thick, and, if all the tales one hears are to be believed, when the cock crows it ambles over to the river for a drink! Fortunately, for those who would prefer not to encounter peripatetic monoliths, there are few cockerels in the vicinity!

A return along the Afon Llia, a delightful walk, will lead unerringly to the picnic area at Blaen Llia.

Route 16.8 Fan Fawr from the Storey Arms Walkers who enjoy long, lonely moorland walks will ascend Fan Fawr from the south, leaving the A4059 at its highest point just north of the minor summit, Cader Fawr. This approach will give a round trip of about 13 kilometres (8 miles), with only the wind, the sheep and buzzards for company. Less stoical individuals will opt for the short, sharp ascent from the Storey Arms Youth Adventure Centre at the top of the A470, and could well be there and back in little more than an hour.

Roadworks carried out during 1983 have obscured the lower part of the Storey Arms' path leading on to Fan Fawr, but the objective is clearly in view with a well-beaten track ascending the final steep section. So the simplest way of dealing with this uncomplicated summit is to choose one's own route to the foot of the track, and to continue steeply from there. The summit is marked by a small stone cairn on the edge of a peaty depression, and gives an excellent view of the Brecon Beacons to the north-east. The trig point shown on OS maps is some distance south-west of the highest point, and should not be confused with it.

DISTANCE: 1.5 kilometres (1 mile)
ASCENT: 295 metres (965 feet)

North of Fan Fawr lies an unnamed summit overlooking the impressive Craig Cerrig-gleisiad, although the crags

The long ridge of Fan Hir.   ▶

are better seen from the A470 near a small picnic area. The continuation northwards to the unnamed summit, while without undue difficulty, requires care in winter on the steep descent from Fan Fawr. Once across the col, from where there is an easy escape route right, back to the Storey Arms, a faint path can be found which eventually winds its way to the two fence-lines and a dilapidated stone wall barring an approach to the edge of the crags. This delineates the boundary of farm land in the centre of which rises Fan Frynych. The landowners, however, are not prepared to give access to this isolated mountain other than by established rights of way, none of which pass over the summit.

It is feasible to make a longer walk by continuing around

The dark summit of Garreg Las seen across the moorland from Foel Fraith. In the distance are the main summits of the Carmarthen Fan.

the grassy watershed to Fan Llia, but on the return journey the need to reach the col north of Fan Fawr may tempt walkers to short cut the return trek across the unnamed summit by contouring directly to the col. This is most strongly advised against; the upper part of the valley feeding the Ystradfellte reservoir is abominably tussocky and not worth the effort in spite of delectable sheltered pools of water in which to bathe aching feet and limbs!

Section 17 – Rhondda

	MAP REFERENCE	HEIGHT (m)	1:50 000 OS MAP
Unnamed summit	906032	600	170

ROUTE
17.1 The unnamed summit by the Coed Morgannwg Way

Between the Rhondda valley, which inspires the hearts and minds of so many Welshmen, and the Vale of Neath to the west is a vast upland area, mainly given over to forestry. The northern extremity of this upland drops severely in a steep escarpment to two small lakes, Llyn Fach and Llyn Fawr, with the highest point of the upland rising between the two. There is no recognised summit name, though the Ordnance Survey use the name, Craig y Llyn. Virtually the whole of this nondescript hill, the lowest 600-metre summit in Wales, is covered with Forestry Commission plantings through which passes a forest trail, the Coed Morgannwg Way, by which the summit is easily reached.

Route 17.1 The unnamed summit by the Coed Morgannwg Way Start from the viewpoint car park at 926031 and walk west, along the edge of the A4061, following a way-marked track – black footprints painted on a white background. The path follows the edge of the escarpment, leaving the road after a short distance and climbing into the forest ahead. Here a broad track through the forest, the Coed Morgannwg Way, is gained, and leads easily to a large cairn, Garn Fach, just off the trail.

A short distance beyond the cairn the trail continues ahead, but turn left, on another track, and ascend slightly to a fire tower and the summit trig point nearby. This is probably the easiest summit in Wales to ascend.

DISTANCE: 2 kilometres (1.25 miles)

ASCENT: 110 metres (360 feet)

Some Welsh place names

Welsh is an ancient, rich and bardic language, but knowing the meaning of just a handful of words will give the walker the component parts of so many place names and, through this, an extra insight into the terrain he is covering. Here are some of the most useful words for hill-walkers.

The top and bottom of things

UCHAF	highest
UWCH	above
AR	on
CANOL (GANOL)	mid
DAN (TAN)	under
IS	below
ISAF	lowest

Size and colour

DU (DDU)	black
GWYN, GWEN (WYN, WEN)	white
LLWYD (LWYD)	grey
COCH (GOCH)	red
GLAS (LAS)	blue, green
GWYRRD (WYRDD)	green
MELYN, MELEN (FELYN, FELEN)	yellow

HIR	long
MAWR (FAWR)	big
BACH, BYCHAN (FACH, FECHAN)	little

Coming down the mountain

PEN	top, head
CNAP	top
BAN (FAN)	peak
CRIB	crest
MYNYDD (FYNYDD)	mountain
BRYN/ARDD	hill
CRAIG (GRAIG)	rock
MAEN	stone
CARN, CARNEDD (GARN, GARNEDD)	cairn
BWLCH	pass
CEFN	whaleback ridge
BRAICH/TRUM	ridge, spur
CLOGWYN	cliff
CRUG	hillock
MOEL (FOEL)	bare hill
BLAEN	highland
ALLT	wooded hillside, cliff
RHIW	hill, slope
RHOS/GWAUN (WAUN)	moorland
FFRIDD	mountain pasture
FFOREST	forest
COED	wood
LLWYN/CELLI (GELLI)	grove
BRO (FRO)	lowland
GWAELOD	foot of hill
TROED	foot
CWM/PANT/GLYN/YSTRAD	valley
CAE/MAES/DÔL	field, meadow

Getting your feet wet

FFYNNON	spring
PISTYLL/RHAEADR	waterfall
PWLL (BWLL)	pool
MELIN (FELIN)	mill
LLYN	lake
NANT	brook
RHYD	ford
AFON	river
PONT (BONT)	bridge
GLAN (LAN)	river bank
CORS (GORS)	bog
ABER	estuary
MORFA	salt marsh
TRAETH	shore
MÔR	sea

An encouraging footnote on pronunciation

Welsh, unlike Scottish or Irish Gaelic, is entirely phonetic. It sounds as it looks. So just have the strength of your convictions and do your best with *ll* and *ch* which are a lot less trouble than the faint-hearted make out.

Just remember seven points:

1 Vowels are shorter, dare one say purer, less drawled than in English.

2 The stress comes on the last syllable but one.

3 *ff* = f and *f* = v

4 *c* and *g* are hard, as in 'conger'

5 *dd* = th, as in 'then' and *th* = th, as in 'thin'

6 *w* is a vowel = oo

7 *y* is a vowel = u, as in 'hut' when alone or anywhere except the final syllable

= i, as in 'hit' in a final syllable
Mynydd (mountain), pronounced mun-ith, with the th of 'then', illustrates the two y sounds. Get *mynydd* right and Welsh-speakers will know you are trying.

Bibliography

The Brecon Beacons National Park, H. D. Westacott (Penguin Books, 1983)

Britannia, William Camden (John Stockdale, 1806, 2nd Ed. Vol. III)

The Drovers' Roads of Wales, Fay Godwin and Shirley Toulson (Wildwood House, 1977)

Eryri, the Mountains of Longing, Amory Lovins (Friends of the Earth, 1972)

Exploring – The Brecon Beacons National Park, Chris Barber (Regional Publications, 1980)

A Guide to Offa's Dyke Path, Christopher John Wright (Constable & Co., 1975)

A Handbook for Travellers in South Wales, (John Murray, New Edition, 1877)

A History of Wales, John Edward Lloyd (Longmans, Green & Co., 1939, 3rd Ed.)

The Industrial Archaeology of Wales, D. Morgan Rees (David & Charles, 1975)

The Journey through Wales, Gerald of Wales (Giraldus Cambrensis) (Penguin Classics, 1978)

Landscapes of North Wales, Roy Millward and Adrian Robinson (David & Charles, 1978)

The Mountains of North Wales, Showell Styles (Gollancz, 1973)

The Mountains of Snowdonia, H. R. C. Carr & G. A. Lister (Crosby Lockwood, 1948, 2nd Ed.)

Mysterious Wales, Chris Barber (David & Charles, 1982)

North Wales, Rev. W. Bingley (Longman & Rees, 1804)

On Foot in North Wales, Patrick Monkhouse (Maclehose & Co., 1934)

Portrait of the Brecon Beacons, Edmund J. Mason (Robert Hale, 1975)

Radnorshire, Lewis Davies (Cambridge University Press, 1912)

Radnorshire, W. H. Howse (E. J. Thurston, 1949)

Rambles in North Wales, Roger Redfern (Robert Hale, 1968)

Snowdon Biography, Young, Sutton & Noyce (J. M. Dent & Sons, 1957)

Snowdonia National Park Guide, No. 2, Ed. Edmund Vale (HMSO, 1958)

The Summits of Snowdonia, Terry Marsh (Robert Hale, 1984)

A Tour in Wales, Thomas Pennant (Henry Hughes, 1783)

Wanderings and Excursions in South Wales, Thomas Roscoe ([1837], London)

Wild Wales, George Borrow (John Murray, ed. 1901)